Adventures in
Self-Directed Learning

WARWICK
SCHOOL

The Library at Warwick School
Please return or renew on or before the last date below

3/19

T & L

STAFF ROOM COLLECTION

D1354131

Adventures in Self-Directed Learning

A Guide for Nurturing Learner Agency and Ownership

BERNARD D. BULL

WIPF & STOCK · Eugene, Oregon

ADVENTURES IN SELF-DIRECTED LEARNING
A Guide for Nurturing Learner Agency and Ownership

Wipf & Stock
An Imprint of Wipf and Stock Publishers
199 W. 8th Ave., Suite 3
Eugene, OR 97401

www.wipfandstock.com

PAPERBACK ISBN: 978-1-5326-1584-9
HARDCOVER ISBN: 978-1-5326-1586-3
EBOOK ISBN: 978-1-5326-1585-6

Manufactured in the U.S.A.   MARCH 16, 2017

"We hold these truths to be self-evident, that all men are created equal, that they are endowed by their Creator with certain unalienable Rights, that among these are Life, Liberty, and the pursuit of Happiness."

Contents

Preface

"I WANT THAT FOR my child!" Less than a year after my daughter's birth, I visited my first project-based learning school, George D. Warriner High School in Sheboygan, Wisconsin. This was near the beginning of a decade-long exploration of diverse models of K-12 and higher education institutions. I wanted to expand my sense of what is possible in teaching and learning, test my assumptions, and more fully consider how we can create far more engaging, humane, and inspiring learning communities. Only a week earlier, I reached out to the principal of this school, and he quickly welcomed me to visit. I observed the students for a short time and spent an hour or two talking with the principal and one of the other teachers.

What I saw and heard stirred my excitement about the possibilities. These were typical high school students who learned the power of taking greater ownership for their learning, gaining a voice in shaping what and how they learn, and the results impressed me. As with any school, it was a work in progress, but it was nonetheless inspiring. There were no traditional classes. Instead, students shared a common course in 21st century skills, but the rest of their learning happened in the form of self-directed student projects, with the guidance and coaching of a teacher.

As I drove home after this visit, I yearned for a school like this for my daughter one day. I wanted a school where students did not just sit in rows and learn to follow instructions, jump through academic hoops, memorize content, strive to get good grades, and learn to be compliant. I wanted a school that would nurture curiosity, a love of learning, a deep and growing sense of agency, ownership, engagement in life and the world, and a strong set of guiding convictions. I wanted a school focused upon helping my daughter and every other student engage in what Paulo Friere called, "the practice of freedom." As Richard Shaull explains in the introduction to Paulo Friere's classic text, *Pedagogy of the Oppressed*:

> There is no such thing as neutral educational process. Education either functions as an instrument that is used to facilitate the integration of the younger generation in the logic of the present system and bring about conformity to it, or it becomes 'the practice of freedom,' the means by which men and women deal critically and creatively with reality and discover how to participate in the transformation of their world. The development of an educational methodology that facilitates this process will inevitably lead to tension and conflict within our society. But it could also contribute to the formation of a new man and mark the beginning of a new era in Western history."[1]

I wanted a school that was less about teaching conformity and more about empowering my daughter and others to find and cultivate their voice. I sought a place where children could learn the freedom, responsibility, and importance of making choices. I dreamt of a classroom where students take pride and ownership in their work, where they engage in inspiring and relevant learning, where their work and learning is the center and not the teacher's performance.

As you will read in the forthcoming chapter, I discovered some of these ideas on my own as a teenager, but I always wondered if there might be a better and more systemic way of helping young people discover the power of being increasingly self-directed learners. My study and visit of such schools confirmed that there is a better way. In fact, there are countless better ways. It just

---

1. Shaull, Introduction to *Pedagogy of the Oppressed*, 34.

depends upon the openness of teachers, students, and others to embrace self-directed learning as an important and increasingly significant part of what happens in school.

My journey started with visiting a few schools like George D. Warriner, but it quickly expanded to a national and even international search. I visited some schools, and I studied even more through primary and secondary resources. I read countless books, interviewed leaders and founders, and in a matter of two or three years, something became apparent. These empowering communities where students learn to shape and own what they learn are far more prevalent than I ever imagined. They are not simple products of an overly utopian imagination. They actually exist. Student learn and thrive in schools committed to self-directed learning, as well as in classrooms where teachers strive to create space in an otherwise traditional school culture to give students an unforgettable taste of taking ownership for their learning. The results might not be documented on formal assessments and standardized tests because few people in education are attempting to measure these sorts of elements. Nonetheless, it is alive and well.

In this book I am going to make a case for self-directed learning as important for individuals but also for our society. How long can a democracy survive if people only learn to comply and they do not learn to speak up about what matters to them and to take ownership for what they accomplish and what happens to them? If students go through years of school where the dominant message is that you get ahead by being submissive and compliant, then I fear that we are doing our students and our communities a disservice.

I wrote about this topic in a chapter about nurturing agency in my book, *What Really Matters? Ten Critical Issues in Contemporary Education*, but this book is a chance for me to expand that conversation in way that will give classroom teachers, homeschooling parents, and others a starting point for action.[2] I am convinced that nurturing agency is among the more critical issues in education today. It ventures into matters of access and opportunity. It touches upon issues of individual rights and responsibilities. In addition,

2. Bull, *What Really Matters?*

it is rooted in the *US Declaration of Independence* and our concept of inalienable rights. This new book, *Adventures in Self-Directed Learning*, is an expansion of that one chapter in the prior book, an opportunity to explore the why of self-directed learning as well as the how of nurturing it.

While my visits to and study of many inspiring alternative schools continue to serve as a vivid illustration of what is possible on a larger scale, I also write this book as a realist. I do not expect every family and community to reinvent school to be more fully student-centered. I realize that standardized tests are not disappearing anytime soon, nor are national and state standards that shape much of the content that students learn. At the same time, none of this means that we cannot work within our existing schools to better nurture self-directed learners. While we might be able to make much faster progress by creating new schools built around these concepts, we can also use our existing classrooms and schools. We can learn to help students take ownership, learn the power and importance of their voice, start to serve as co-designers of their learning, and to play more of a direct role in deciding what, how, and why they learn. We can do this in any classroom, granted that the teacher and students are willing to give it a try.

As such, I write this book primarily for the teachers and other stakeholders who find themselves in more traditional school environments, but wo also see a need for at least some measure of change if we are going to prepare students to thrive in this connected age. I offer it as an opportunity to consider why we might want to focus upon nurturing agency and self-direction. I provide this book to help readers consider a few ways to get started nurturing self-directed learners next week and next year. This is not a "how to" book that gives readers a systematic guide on how to build a self-directed learning classroom or school, but I worked hard to make it something that is not just philosophical. I am hopeful that readers will find this to be a healthy blend of philosophical ideas and more applied tips, because both are necessary.

Consider this book a potential launch pad into what I hope will become a lifelong adventure in self-directed learning.

While I do not expect every reader to agree with everything that I write (in fact that would be concerning), I openly admit that I am writing to persuade. Amid my study and observation, I see the power of possibility of self-directed learning, not simply as a method of teaching, but especially as a mindset of living. I believe that it is important for individuals but also for society. I believe that giving more attention to this topic can create schools that are, in the words of Paulo Friere, more humanizing. As such, it is my hope and prayer that readers will, at least in small ways, come to see the wisdom in the following quote from John Holt:

> What is essential is to realize that children learn independently, not in bunches; that they learn out of interest and curiosity, not to please or appease the adults in power; and that they ought to be in control of their own learning, deciding for themselves what they want to learn and how they want to learn it."[3]

I know that many read such a quote, especially teachers facing the realities of the modern teaching profession and classroom, and they find themselves insisting on pointing out any number of important caveats. There can be the temptation to take this idea of self-directed learning, analyze it in its most extreme form, and then feel justified in dismissing it altogether. I truly hope that this book offers an alternative. Teachers can make a difference in their classrooms. They can experience the great joy of watching their students grow and learn, developing the competence and confidence to play more active roles in their learning. Then teachers can follow these students over the years as they grow to become able, confident, self-reliance agents of positive change in their own lives, their communities, and beyond.

3. Holt, *How Children Learn*, 290.

1

What is Self-Directed Learning?

WHAT DO ABRAHAM LINCOLN, Benjamin Franklin, Thomas Edison, Nikola Tesla, and Leonardo da Vinci have in common? Yes, they were influential or successful in one or more ways and they are household names today, but there is something more to them. There is something about them that can help us flourish, something that can help learners thrive in our increasingly connected world. They were deeply curious, they had a love of learning, and they had a sense of personal agency. They believed that they could control how they learned and what they learned. They were self-directed learners. It was that belief and capacity for self-direction that I believe catapulted them into the history books. They built upon their gifts. In doing so, each made a difference in the world. As such, one of the questions, perhaps the key question for this book is this: *How can we help more learners embrace a self-directed approach to life and learning?*

A related, second question is this: *How can we nurture a growing sense of competence and confidence in young people so that they step up to the challenges of their time, and stand up for their deepest convictions in the modern world?* In *Adventures in Self-Directed Learning,* I draw from two decades of study to help explore how we can better nurture competent, confident, curious, creative, collaborative, courageous young people who are ready to face the challenges and embrace the opportunities of life and learning in a connected and digital age.

For me, this journey started a long time ago. I think back to three distinct experiences: the first in my late teens, the second occurred in college, and the third occurred just after graduating from college. Each one took me a little deeper into this world of self-directed learning. As such, I want to start this book by telling you a little bit of that story, because this is not just a book about another educational topic. This is a cause that grows from my own life and experiences.

The First Experience

When I was in my late teens, my high school physics teacher invited me to house sit for him during the summer. The prospect of a little independence sounded like great fun so I took him up on the offer. That summer was also right after my first year of college, and I unfortunately suffered an injury on the college basketball team that required surgery. I finished the season, but during that summer of house sitting (and taking some classes at the local University), I had the surgery and then spent my summer recovering. For me, summer was often filled with manual labor jobs and plenty of basketball, but I was in for a summer of sitting around, at least for a month or two.

I settled into his basement by the television and watched a few videos, but you can only watch so much television. Then I browsed the shelves of books that he had on one wall. I can say with confidence that I had not read a single book on those shelves. I can say that because, up to that point in life, I did not read much of anything, but that was about to change. I picked up a copy of a book by Stephen Hawking, *A Brief History of Time*.[1] I read the back cover, browsed the table of contents, and I wanted more.

Books always played an important role in my life. We did not have many books in my home growing up, but I always thought of

---

1. Hawking and Runger. *A Brief History of Time*.

reading as a gateway to new worlds and ideas, a means of creating new opportunities for people. In a book, you could travel the world without leaving your living room. Depending upon your age, such a message might sound familiar because there was a time in the 1980s and 1990s where there seemed to be an especially concentrated number of commercials and efforts to promote reading for children. As such, my interest in books probably came from watching literacy advertisements during Saturday morning cartoons, or maybe teachers who challenged us to read more. While I loved the idea of reading, I did not do it. I spent time with friends. I loved talking about ideas with people. I thrived on tinkering and taking things apart, although I often never got them back together. I also loved basketball. Yet, in all of those interests, reading did not make the list.

Holding that Stephen Hawking text, I decided to start reading, not just that book, but I wanted to read as many books as possible. As such, I set the goal of trying to read a book a day. I started early in the morning, read through much of the day, and tried to finish the book by bedtime. I cannot say for certain that I actually read a full book every single day, but that is how I remember it, and I know that I read countless books, including a fair amount of science fiction, something that was brand new to me. In one summer, I read more books than I did in the prior eighteen years.

That summer of reading changed me. I developed an insatiable appetite for books and reading. I bought books at garage sales. I scoured the discard piles at libraries, and I read anything that interested me, mostly nonfiction. I read across subjects and disciplines. I scribbled questions and quotes in random notebooks. This turned into the most intellectually engaging time of my life up to that point.

When the summer ended, my love for reading continued. I applied for a job at the college library when I returned to college the next school year, which provided me with a first pick of any discarded books or book donations that didn't fit the library's needs. I had a collection of hundreds of books by the end of the next year. I dreamt about what I read, talked about the ideas with anyone who would listen, and found my mind to be a far more interesting place.

In fact, I attribute reading to giving me a more accessible and spacious internal life. Before I read frequently, I vividly remember the frustration of trying to grapple with big ideas, but I could not see them or make sense of them. I did not have the stories or vocabulary to help me understand these ideas and how they related to one another. I felt like a professional musician who was tone deaf and could not read music. I had the passion but I did not have the skill to turn that passion into something beautiful. Yet, as I read more books, I began to build a collection of stories, words, concepts, and mental tools that allowed me to think more deeply and with more clarity about those haunting ideas of old, not to mention countless new ideas. Even to this day, I value processing my thoughts through talking and writing, but I believe that reading widely also expanded my capacity to ponder ideas and life; and I am incredibly grateful for that gift.

As such, it was not just about the knowledge gained through the books. Just as transformational was the fact that I was managing and directing my own learning. I was going to the library and picking out books of interest. This was not something coming for a course assignment, parent direction, or a teacher's request. I came across something that intrigued me, and I pursued it. I asked questions and then sought out books that might aid me in deepening my understanding of the question, and maybe even discovering some answers. I consider this the beginning of my life as a self-directed learner. In the past, I thought of schooling and learning as synonymous, but no longer. I began to see learning as this wonderfully self-directed endeavor that can happen in and out of school. It was not something that I did for a test or grade. I did it because my curiosity compelled me. Learning became something that I did, not something done to me by a teacher. Of course, many teachers played the role of mentor and knowledgeable resource, and helpful guide; but the teacher was no longer an essential ingredient of a learning experience. As I am known to say and write, the only essential ingredients in a learning experience are learning and an experience. Other ingredients add flavor, and they may well be important in many situations. Nonetheless, as one grows as a confident and competent self-directed learner, there is a sober discovery that the role of teacher is valuable but increasingly less necessary over time.

I contend that most great teachers embrace this reality. The goal is not to educate people who are perpetually dependent upon the teacher to learn. The goal is to equip learners who are increasingly independent, eventually capable of directing their own learning.

To be fair and honest, most who recall me as a student will tell you that I was always curious. Remember that kid in the room who used to ask constant questions? Remember how he got on your nerves at times because he didn't always recognize his boundaries? Remember wishing that he would just be quiet so you could listen and take the notes that you needed for the test? I was that annoying, question-filled student.

The difference of discovering self-selected and self-directed reading was that I discovered a new outlet for this curiosity. It led to countless other avenues for learning in the future, but this also helped me gain some self-control in the classroom. Even today, I still ask plenty of questions, but now the classroom is just one of a growing number of ways to ask questions and discover answers.

I believe that this is possible for any learner. There will be different levels of curiosity from one student to another. Some will embrace self-direction more fully and more quickly than others. Yet, in our increasingly connected age, I believe that this is a mindset and skillset that will enhance the life and learning of all students.

The Second Experience

Remember that college library job that I just mentioned in the last section? That led to a second self-directed learning epiphany. That library became a home base for my next discovery as a self-directed learner. I went to a wonderful liberal arts college in Wisconsin where I took classes from full-time, often brilliant, and almost always present professors. I did not have a single class taught by a graduate assistant, for example; and it was the rare exception for me to have a part-time instructor. These full-time faculty welcomed students during office hours, including visits from students who were not enrolled in their classes, and I took full advantage of that. Some even invited me over to their houses for dinner.

On any given week, I visited three or four different professors, not to ask for help on a specific assignment or in preparation for a test. I wanted to learn from them. I wanted their advice on ideas that haunted me (in a good way) as a result of my newly developed reading habit. While my frequent visits started to exhaust some faculty, they were gracious and I learned as much from these visits as I did in any class. In fact, that was an epiphany for me, and I decided to formalize my learning outside of class.

At some point in college, I decided that it was time for me to take even greater ownership for my learning. I tried to do a decent job in my classes, writing papers and preparing for exams; but that was not enough for me. I decided to start giving myself writing assignments. I picked a question of interest, scanned the books and resources in the library, and starting writing weekly to bi-weekly research papers for myself. When finished, I placed the new paper in a folder for future use. Over time, I gathered a large enough collection of papers and notes that, when I started a new course and read the syllabus, it was not uncommon for me to have a ready-made paper to submit a formal assignment. It did not always work out that easily, and some have since claimed that this practice was unethical. I did not think of it that way. I saw it as blending the formal school requirements with my personal curriculum and goals. I learned a great deal from these combined papers and projects, and even more about myself as a learner.

There are obvious limitations to this early experiment. I did not get feedback from others on most of what I wrote, only the papers that I eventually turned in for a class. That lack of feedback meant that the quality of my work only went so far. Nonetheless, this became an opportunity for me to cultivate a wonderfully intrinsic motivation for learning, and it served me well in my later work, in my aspirations to be a writer, and when I arrived in graduate school.

In graduate school, where student voice and choice played a much larger role, I noticed some classmates struggle with this new expectation of autonomy. For me, it fit perfectly what the habits that I cultivated through more self-directed reading and writing. Even more important to me, this set me on the path to discovering some my life work and passions.

This idea of a college student giving himself assignments might sound rare and outrageous, but in our connected age, this sort of thing is increasingly common for learners. They might not go to a physical library and write papers, but they are feeding their curiosity and engaging in learning outside of formal school. Some are learning to code and connecting with others online. Others are nurturing their love of literature and writing through fan fiction websites. Others spend countless hours watching inspirational but educational videos that explore everything from neuroscience to how to bake a cake.

The readily available learning resources and communities on the web are a game changer for 21st century learning. The strange aberration of me writing papers for myself is now present in countless young people who are going online to ask questions that are often less welcome in class. Some are taking advantage of this more than others, but that is part of this purpose of this book. I contend that this common behavior is something that we can nurture and celebrate in our schools, and that it will help schools achieve their goals while also further empowering learners to set and reach their personal goals as well. The blending of learning in the classroom and learning outside of the classroom is one of the more significant changes of our generation.

The Third Experience

When I was only a few months out of college, I had an experience that expanded my view of self-directed learning once more. I was reading a book, *Frames of Mind*, by Howard Gardner. It is the book where Gardner introduced the concept of multiple intelligences to the broader world.[2] In fact, before reading that book, I found a draft of a paper that Gardner wrote on the idea of multiple intelligences. It included a message that it was in draft form and should not be cited in formal papers. Yet, the ideas in that paper turned into a book that put forth one of the most influential psychological theories in education of the last century. As I read it, I had a number of questions. This was in the 1990s and I wished that I could talk to Howard Gardner, but I did not go to Harvard where he taught, I did not live nearby, and I did not know him personally. Looking over at my computer—it was actually the first computer that I bought with my own money, I realized, "I bet that I could find Howard Gardner online." I got online and did not Google him; I think I AltaVisted him because that was my search engine of choice at the time. I found Harvard's website. I located his contact information. I reached out to him. I did not get a personal email from Howard Gardner, but I did get a reply from one of his graduate assistants with the job of helping reply to his email inquiries. I also received answers to my questions within two days.

In a moment, a book became a two-way conversation with the author (or at least the author's graduate assistant). I developed this sense that I was connected to authors, in real-time potentially, and that became a lifetime journey for me. Now, when I am learning something new, I ask questions like the following: Who are the leading experts in the world, and how can I connect to them? Are there people doing interesting or promising work in this area with whom I could speak? How can I learn from them? How can I connect with them? That was a seismic shift in my learning, and it introduced me to this world of self-directed learning in a connected age that we are going to explore together in this book.

As we will explore further, some think that self-directed learning is some sort of solitary learning, and that is usually far from reality. Instead, it is a wonderfully connected and collaborative form of learning. It is just that the learners are setting at least

2. Gardner, *Frames of Mind*.

some of the goals and co-designing some or all of the learning pathways. In fact, if someone fails to develop this ability to direct one's own learning by building connections, I worry that they will be at a disadvantage in this digital age.

Self-Directed Learning Defined

It occurred to me recently that, while I have been writing and talking about self-directed learning for over a decade, this is not a familiar term to many in education or beyond. Or even if people have a general sense of the term, they are not necessarily informed about the broader conversation and understanding of what different people mean by it. As such, allow me to take couple steps back and offer some working definitions for self-directed learning.

At first glance, self-directed learning could be interpreted as solitary learning, independent learning, teacher-less learning, and a dozen other things. It can include any of those elements and more. It is a concept that has relevance when you are exploring learning outside of formal schooling, within traditional schools, as well as the myriad of learning communities online, in the workplace, in churches, and throughout our communities.

To help dispel myths and generate more productive thinking about the value of self-directed learning, I propose two working definitions for self-directed learning. Both are by thought leaders in this area. The first, by Malcolm Knowles, is over 40 years old, and originally had adult learners in mind. The second has a history as well, but it is more current and includes a broader set of learners.

Knowles defined self-directed learning in this way: "Broadly, as a process in which individuals take the initiative with or without the help of other[s], to diagnose their learning needs, formulate learning goals, identify resources for learning, select and implement learning strategies, and evaluate learning outcomes."[3]

3. Knowles, *Self-Directed Learning*, 18.

Knowles popularized this common definition for self-directed learning, and his definition is still among one of the most quoted in the academic literature. He used it to focus on his primary area of interest, adult learning. Some used his writing and ideas for younger learners, but that was not the target audience. For decades (and even today), people argue that this concept of self-directed learning is better suited for the adult learner, arguing that younger learners are neither capable nor developmentally ready for doing what Knowles describes in this definition.

In more recent conversations about self-directed learning, some educators believe that this is an "approach" to teaching that is better suited for gifted and talented learners. This gifted learning emphasis is not the case with Knowles. His definition is useful and important because his definition and application was certainly not focused upon a small, élite group of minds. It is a concept applied to a broad set of adult learners ranging from formal higher education to continuing education, informal learning to continuing and community education. Anyone is capable of progressing toward greater levels of self-direction.

If we look at Knowles' definition as representing a spectrum, we can see that an environment need not be entirely self-directed or absent of self-direction. It is possible for learners and teachers to partner in identifying learning needs, setting goals, planning the learning experiences and monitoring progress toward learning. In one circumstance, the teacher might set the goals and plan each detail of the learning activities and assessments. In another, the learners might have some input on one of those elements. In yet another context or at the "right time," the learner might be a true partner with the teacher and classmates in designing one or more of those elements. Finally, at a time and context of great learner independence, the learner might be in full or nearly full control, using the teacher simply as a guide or coach on occasion. As such, we can benefit from thinking about degrees of self-directed learning and not just labeling something as self-directed or not.

This is an important point because there are proponents of self-directed learning who scoff at anything that resembles adult direction. They argue that it is not self-directed learning unless the teachers are absent, silent, or play at small of a role as reasonably possible. That is certainly one side of the spectrum for self-directed learning, but you do not need to agree with that extreme to take advantage of self-directed learning. There are more modest or moderate approaches that we can use to enhance learning in even the most traditional and teacher-directed environments. In fact, while I believe that this book is valuable for people at any point on that spectrum, I am writing it with extra attention to those more moderate-minded people. I am a champion for moving toward as much learner independence as is reasonable for a given context. At the same time, I also know that a teacher in a traditional classroom can take some of these ideas and apply them in ways that empower learners, enhance the overall learner experience, and better prepare learners for the type of self-direction that will set them up for success in a connected world.

Advocates of self-directed learning argue that at least creating a progression toward this type of learner independence is important. It represents a collection of skills that are valuable, sometimes critical, for independence and a high degree of agency in the rest of life. Survey a random group in society and you will likely discover that most people agree with this idea. Where we disagree is in considering the best pathway(s) to helping learners become independent and more self-directed.

A common myth related to defining self-directed learning is that it is somehow inherently anti-teacher. In a sense, that is correct on one far side of the self-directed learning spectrum. Yet, for many, even most, that is a myth. In a chapter in *The Sourcebook of Self-Directed Learning* (edited by Rothwell and Sensenig), Hiemstra explains it this way when writing about self-directed learning in training environments. "SDL calls for trainers to adopt new roles. SDL does not mean that trainers are superfluous and that trainees should learn everything in a sink-or-swim manner. Instead, in SDL, trainers enact such important roles as: facilitator, enabling agent, and resource agents."[4] The difference is where we

4. Hiemstra, "Self-Directed Learning," 6.

place the power. Self-directed learning is about empowering the learners, equipping them to take control of their learning more and more as time passes.

Adding a stronger editorial comment, my greatest concern is not when formal education is heavily teacher-centered, but when there is no intentional planning or vision for helping learners progress toward independence. This is a shortsighted and short-term approach to education. It is only concerned with what students "need to learn" about a given content area and not how to equip learners to grow as self-regulated, self-motivated lifelong learners. Learning how to learn, experiencing the joy of learning, and developing effective habits as a learner are important enough to call for a national conversation.

This is important whether we are teaching elementary school children or doctoral students. As an example, consider the difference in quality between doctoral programs. Some programs only accept highly self-directed learners. Others accept capable but dependent learners, but they do not help these dependent learners progress toward the independence needed to succeed on a thesis or dissertation (having a high non-completion rate). Still others have changed doctoral programs to make them more step-by-step, helping people finish, but never really learning how to be a self-regulated and independent researcher and scholar. They graduate with a terminal degree and are not that much more self-directed than when they started. If that happens on the highest levels of education, how much more do we face this challenge in the elementary, secondary, and undergraduate higher education levels?

A second definition for self-directed learning comes from Maurice Gibbons. His definition broadens the scope from adult learners to learners of any age. "Self-directed learning is any increase in knowledge, skill, accomplishment or personal development that an individual selects and brings about by his or her own efforts, using any method, in any circumstances, at any time."[5]

This is a less tactical definition than what we see with Knowles' definition, but there are similarities. What they have in

---

5. Gibbons, *The Self-Directed Learning Handbook*, 2.

common is that self-directed learning is about the learner building competence and confidence to become more than a passive recipient of learning. The learners are active agents, even directors of their own learning. What I appreciate about Gibbons' definition is that it contrasts self-directed learning with other forms of learning by focusing upon one key component. It is by the learner's "own efforts." At the same time, the "any circumstances, at any time" part of the definition allows us to recognize that self-directed learning is not limited to one context or setting, one type of school or program. The self-directed learner can make use of any method or circumstance, including traditional teacher-directed learning environments. It is not the context that makes it self-directed as much as the learner. What makes it self-directed is that the learner "selects and brings about . . . the increase in knowledge, accomplishment or personal development."

I have never spoken directly with Gibbons about this, but his definition has the breadth to help us see self-directed learning as beginning with learner agency. The learner is the agent, not just a recipient. In mandatory K-12 public school settings, this might be difficult to see. Yet, even in such mandatory settings, the enlightened learners can still recognize that they have final say on what, if, how, and why they learn. They might choose to submit to the instructions and guidance of a teacher. They might not. They might also blend some of their own goals and strategies with that of the teacher. Some learners do not perceive this as a choice. This might seem like splitting hairs, but learner choice is always present in learning environments unless that environment is using extreme propaganda, manipulation, or brainwashing techniques. I like to think that such techniques are the rare exception in education today. As such, what I am saying here almost certainly applies to the context of anyone who is reading this book.

Both of these definitions give us a helpful starting point for thinking and talking about self-directed learning. As with most terms in education, there is not uniform agreement or universal usage of a single definition. In fact, on more than one occasion, readers of my online articles about self-directed learner have called me out on my approach to the subject. In some cases, they did not think that I went far enough. In other cases, I they thought my ideas too extreme. Some saw my characterization as "self-directed learning light." Others saw it as verging on anarchy. There is plenty of room for all of us in this modern education ecosystem. Yet, these two definitions provide enough clarity for us to have fruitful conversations and to consider how we might nurture or at least leave room for the growth and development of self-direction.

When we become more self-directed, the question moves from the teacher to the student. With a teacher-directed class, it is the teacher who asks, "What do I want or need the students to learner?" As we progress toward self-direction, there come times when there is room for students to ask, "What do I need or want to learn?" A second question that a teacher might ask is, "How will I know when the students have met the learning goal?" That leads teachers to create some kind of assignment, assessment or test to measure student learning. They need some means of measuring student progress and learning. From the more self-directed stand-point, we invite the students into helping answer that question. Students ask questions like the following. How will I know if I have learned and how will I show what I learned? How will I document it? How will I be able to demonstrate to myself and to others that I met this goal and that I learned something significant? Learners are challenged to come up with answers to these questions, at least to some extent.

Yet another question in a teacher-centered context is this. How will I help the students get there? How will I teach them or help them learn? This is where teachers start thinking about the design of the lesson, the learning experience, or the learning pathway. As you might expect, we flip that as we progress toward self-direction. Learners start to ask learning pathway questions. How am I going to get there? How am I going to learn this? What do I need to do? What resources do I need? What strategies, what practices, what experiences do I need? What do I have to do in order to reach this goal, to show and know that I learned this?

It is inspiring to see learners take such ownership for helping to design the pathways to their learning goals. Yet, for most learners, this does not happen instantly. They must learn how to learn. They must discover what constitutes more and less effective learning pathways. As such, the learners start to develop expertise in goal setting, lesson designing, content curation, and building feedback or assessment plans for themselves. As anyone who trained to become a teacher knows, this takes time and practice; but it is achievable to some degree for all learners.

I will add one final question that is part of this mix as well. Good teachers ask this. They ask the question, "How am I going to make sure I know how students are doing along the way?" This is about monitoring student progress, checking their understanding so that we can step in and help them if they are going astray or struggling too much. Or, if they are making progress, we might choose to share an encouraging word. Again, from the self-directed learning standpoint, this now becomes a question for the learners. "How am I going to know how I am doing? How am I going to check my own progress and understanding?"

This last question is critical because we know that very little learning happens without feedback. Imagine trying to get good at hitting the target with a bow and arrow blindfolded. You are unable to see or hear whether you hit the target. You keep shooting arrow after arrow in what you think is the correct direction. Without feedback, how are you supposed to know how you are doing? How are you going to how when, if, and how to adjust what you are doing to improve your performance? Without some sort of feedback it is nearly impossible to learn. That feedback might be so natural and embedded that we do not see it as feedback, but there need to be some mechanism for guiding your practice and improvement. Since this is such a critical element of learning, imagine the power of equipping students with the knowledge and skill to design their own feedback loops, to elicit feedback from various available sources. This is truly equipping people for life-long learning.

What is Self-Blended Learning?

At times in this book, I will mention yet another term, self-blended learning. This is really just a creative combination of two terms, blended learning and self-directed learning. I find that it helps some people and is confusing for others. If it helps you, great. If not, then do not worry about it. When you see the phrase self-blended learning, just replace it in your mind with self-directed learning, because the former is just a subset of the latter. Yet, I find this distinction a powerful one for those who are trying to take ideas about self-directed learning and apply them to a more traditional learning context, so I will at least introduce it at this point in the book.

The real shift here in self-directed learning is that we are trying to empower and encourage the learners to own the learning. Self-blended learning is essentially blended learning (which I will define in the following pages) plus self-directed learning. Advocates of self-blended learning are especially interested in ways that students are self-directing, but they are doing in more traditional schooling environments, sometimes even apart from the teacher's guidance. Students might be in a traditional, teacher-directed high school social studies class. Yet, for one of many possible reasons, the students choose to expand on what the teacher planned. The students supplement or enhance their learning about social studies. It might come from curiosity about a topic mentioned in the class. It might come from the students wanting more feedback and guidance than is currently available in the class. Whatever the case, the students use digital or other resources to enhance or expand the learning in some way.

Self-blended learning is taking self-directed learning that I already mentioned and combining it with the notion of blended learning. There are countless definitions for blended learning but at its foundation, blending learning is about combining face-to-face and digital learning, something that is commonplace in most classrooms. There might be in-class activities combined with online digital content and resources. There could be online video clips blended with in-class discussions. There are settings where students rotate through different stations at school, one station being student work at a computer on some sort of educational software followed by the next station where the student gets small group mentoring and guidance from a teacher.

There are countless ways for this to take place, but it is usually the teacher in charge of the blending. The teacher is selecting and curating online content and resources. The teacher is choosing the software and online learning experiences. The teacher is choosing when and how to blend face-to-face and online learning. Yet, the idea of self-blended learning, at least as I am using it here, is that the student begins to play a greater role in finding and using various digital resources to enhance the otherwise teacher-directed learning experience. The student turns to Khan Academy to help understand a concept taught in class. Another student might be in a writing class, but she discovers an online group of aspiring teenage authors who meet online weekly to give each other encouragement and feedback on one another's work. Still another student seeks out additional readings and experts online to learn more about the subject introduced in class.

What is distinct about what I am describing is that the student is now the one doing much of the blending, not just the teacher. This is already happening in classes around the world. It does not require teacher intervention. In fact, teachers are sometimes completely unaware that it is taking place. Yet, this skill of learning to enhance and supplement your learning is also a powerful skill for life in a connected world. The people who develop the confidence and competence to do this will gain a major advantage in the workplace and many other areas of life.

2

Why Self-Directed Learning?

WITHOUT A COMPELLING REASON, why would anyone go through the hard work of encouraging and fostering self-directed learning in a school? This is not easy work. It takes time and energy, even emotional energy, to build a learning community where self-directed learning is valued and commonplace. As such, this is a chapter focused upon examining a few of the many reasons for embracing the challenge of this hard work.

Student Voice

We need people who will stand up for what is right in the world. We need people who know how to learn and listen from others, but who also have the courage to stand up and be heard. How can a democratic nation survive if we do not have that? When people talk about school as a place to equip good citizens, we sometimes forget that this is not just about fostering compliant rule-followers who also happen to vote. We also want people to know how to stand up, speak up, effect change, and be influencers in their communities, country, and world. We want people to have voices and use them, and school is a place where we can help students find that voice. It is just that we might need to reconsider how we go about a few things. Self-directed learning is a great starting point.

What voices do students actually have in most learning organizations? What are our biases and assumptions about student voice? What happens when we move from education as something done to students to something that students do themselves? What amazing visions for education could we make a reality if we tapped into the perspectives and brilliance of young people in our K-12 and higher education institutions?

Ask a group of educators how to solve a problem and, more often than not, we will suggest some sort of educational solution. We are wired that way. Ask a sociologist and you will get a sociological answer. Ask a psychologist and you get a psychological answer. Ask a theologian about a social problem and there is a good chance that you will get a theological answer. They will look at it from their distinct lens and provide a sociological, psychological or theological assessment, drawing from solutions most common in their fields. What does this mean for how we aspire to find solutions to education's greatest challenges today?

Interestingly, there is a voice that is often muffled in education. More often than not, these people are not involved in hiring decisions; exploration of new possibilities; plans for quality improvement; innovations in teaching, learning and curriculum; along with broader aspirations to address the digital divide, access and opportunity, workforce development, and more. We rarely involve the students.

In 1995, Kathryn Church wrote a groundbreaking book about mental health called *Forbidden Narratives: Critical Autobiography as Social Science*. Unlike many other books about mental health, this text included the author's own lived experiences, finding herself in the curious position of being both a mental health professional and a mental health patient. Reading this lived experience of a researcher and patient changed the trajectory of my work and research. She introduced me to the important world of auto-ethnography and autobiography as research.[1]

This research method continues to be challenged by more than a few in the social sciences, but for me, it opened my eyes to

1. Church, *Forbidden Narratives*.

the fact that much research fails to take us deeply into the lived experiences of people from their own perspectives. Researchers, as much as we try, paint the picture of other people's lived experiences, but we hold the paintbrush. Apart from select excerpts that illustrate a theme or concept, the subjects do not have an opportunity to be heard, not directly. It is a controlled and systematic reporting of the findings from the researcher's standpoint, but it does not necessarily represent the nuance and voice of each subject in the study. Some researchers are better at this than others, but they rarely achieve what can be experienced when we hear directly from those subjects.

Applying this lesson from Church's work, I contend that we have the same challenge as we pursue opportunities and innovations in education. We survey students. We might run focus groups. We observe and analyze student motivation, engagement, persistence, learning, and more. We are collecting more data about our students than at any other time in history. Far less often do we invite the students into designing the schools, curriculum, and courses. How often do they help shape what, how, when or where they learn? How do we engage them in prioritizing, budgeting, establishing policy and practice?

Some argue that it is unwise to engage the learners in such important work, that it is best left to the expert educationists or academic professionals. Yet, look at higher education institutions around the world and academics are making educational decisions when they often have little to no formal training in the field of education. Policy makers are making important decisions that shape the future of education when many have done little to read, research, and study deeply in the areas that they are influencing. Even those trained in education are consistently making educational decisions based on their personal experience or preferences as much or more than their study of the research or by tapping into a solid body of evidence-based practice. Given these realities, why would it be out of line to empower students to own not only their learning but the communities in which they learn?

The good news is that this is happening, even if in small ways. When I visited Western Sydney University, I saw this beautiful University library rich with collaborative spaces, study spaces, "silent" spaces, and even a sleep pod for those students needing a quick nap between a day of work and evening classes. When I asked about the design decisions, I learned that the students had an active say in much of it. In fact, there is a portion of the annual library budget controlled by the students. This allows them to pursue ongoing innovations, creating study spaces that align with their needs.

In classrooms and schools around the United States, school leaders and teachers invite students to establish and shape everything from classroom rules to what and how they will learn. This is especially true in many schools embracing the self-directed learning movement making its way around the world. If you visit Acton Academy in Austin, Texas, you would learn that students establish many of the rules. They provide peer assessments. They work together to keep the facilities clean. They have ample say in what and how they learn. They even get to help create some of the learning experiences. When I visited Acton Academy in 2015, I was impressed by the sense of agency and ownership displayed by each student.

Learning about the original formation of KM Global, a project-based and personalized learning charter school in Wisconsin, Dr. Valerie Schmitz explained that much of the original vision for the school came from a team of students that she consulted. She gathered high school students to join her in developing the vision for the school that eventually turned into its initial charter.[2]

How does a teacher or learning organization get serious about this? We will explore that question in many ways throughout the rest of this book, but for those who are anxious to get started, here are some initial ideas to consider.

1. Create a team of students who help make decisions about the physical spaces in the learning organization.

2. Have a combined team of students, teachers, and other related stakeholders to meet four or more times a year to plan

2. Valerie Schmitz, October 8, 2015.

key curricular innovations, including school-wide projects and timely elements of the curriculum.

3. Involve student voice in the interview process of new employees ranging from administrators and janitorial staff to teachers and coaches.

4. For secondary and higher education especially, have a student advisory committee for each department, division, college, or school.

5. Create a means of obtaining formal feedback from the students about the school culture, curriculum, and experience at least once a week.

6. Encourage teachers to establish small teams of students that work with the teacher to design, revise, and adjust lessons and units as the school year progresses.

7. In formal and intentional ways, invite and create specific ways for students to become growing experts on teaching and learning research and practice.

8. When new projects, innovations, practices, models, and resources are being considered; have teams of students play an active role in the research, review, and decision. In fact, why not have a means by which students can propose and initiate such things?

Student voice matters in education today. Listening to those voices and, even more, entrusting students with decisions about the nature of their learning communities, has tremendous benefits. I am not just referring to benefits in terms of test score results and measurable academic gains. What if we also look at the benefits of creating more equitable and humane learning communities for today? We see this happening in promising ways, but what if we saw it even more? What if we found ways to persistently engage students in tackling some of education's greatest challenges and pursuing some of its greatest opportunities? What if the students had more room to imagine the possibilities and to pursue them?

Access & Opportunity

An education can be a rich and rewarding experience. It is not, however, a magical solution to access & opportunity. The more that I learn about promising possibilities in formal K-12 and higher education, the more I become convinced that an emphasis on curiosity, a love of learning, agency, and capacity for self-direction are among some of the best investments of our time and resources in education reform. This is because even the most elite lecture halls are not the solution to issues of educational access and opportunity. I offer an early personal college experience as a way of illustrating this point.

My first year in college I had a 7:30 AM American civilization class. The class met in a room a few hundred feet from my dormitory. Since the entire University, with the exception of one building, was connected by hallways, I did not have to go outside to get to class. I would set my alarm for 7:25 AM, put on sandals, and wander into class a minute or two early.

Given the day and time, this class was where I experienced my first college exam. The entire class consisted of one paper, a midterm exam, and a final exam; so I had not received any feedback from the instructor before this first test. I never even had a one-on-one conversation with him. I completed about half of the assigned readings, made it to class every session (albeit half asleep), took notes as best as I knew how at the time, and that was about it. The content intrigued me, but not as much as the important challenge of building new friendships and experiencing college community from 8:00 PM to 2:00 AM almost every night. I arrived on the morning of my first college test having reviewed my notes for about an hour, assuming that was adequate for the task. He handed out something that he called a Blue Book, a 5x7 empty collection of sixteen lined pages of paper. He wrote a few essay questions on the board and told us to begin.

I did not know what to do. One of the questions on the board did not trigger any memories from the readings, lectures, or notes. A second related to a topic that piqued my interest in an earlier lecture, but my knowledge of the details was limited. The third was familiar from high school American history class where I wrote a research paper on the subject. I started with the familiar question and easily scribbled (if you ever saw my handwriting, you would commend me for such a precise word choice) four or five pages of an answer. I struggled through the essay for the second question, but there was only so much that I could do. It was not like I could work harder at recalling the necessary insights because they did not exist in my brain. I had an interested but shallow knowledge of the subject. Then there was the third question. I do not know what I wrote, but it was not good. As class came to an end, I set my Blue Book on the table in the front of class and headed to a late morning breakfast.

Skip ahead to 7:30 AM, the next time that we met for class. I showed up, listened to the lecture, took notes, and then he returned the graded exams during the last five minutes of class. I opened my book and found a "B-" marked at the top. I scanned the pages and counted a total of twenty words of comments, most of which consisted of phrases like "more detail" or "inaccurate."

Two months later, I was better prepared for the final exam. I even showed up earlier than usual. As I waited for the test to start, I mumbled a few words to the person next to me, explaining how I studied but had no idea if I was ready for this test, alluding to the belief that the professor was largely to blame. I did not expect such a strong reaction from the classmate, a senior who must have switched majors along the way or somehow missed this introductory class earlier in his college career. He was a football player and I never talked to him before. I had seen him in a completely different state on Friday nights after enjoying the party scene off campus, but he seemed surprisingly serious at the moment. He was not pleased with my critique of the professor, leaned toward me, and retorted with three simple questions. Did you read? Did you study? How long did you study? There was no time for me to answer before the professor arrived and the exam started.

This classmates's reply represented a belief about what it takes to be successful in college. It has less to do with the professor and almost everything to do with the student. Students who read, think, study, and work hard within the parameters set by the instructor earn the best grades. The professor lectures, creates tests and assignments, and grades the quality of your work.

Over the entire semester, I never had a one-on-one conversation with the professor. Thinking back, this might have set the groundwork for my growing interest in self-directed learning in a connected world. In some ways, it did not set the bar very high for independent learning. If I could find quality content and a person or group of people to give me rich and substantive feedback on my progress, I would have met or exceeded what I experienced in this first year American civilization class.

The first year of college consisted of the largest class sizes with the least amount of personal feedback and interaction with the professor. Later years involved ample small seminars, rich and rewarding one-on-one conversations with professors, robust peer discussion in and out of class, and even a good measure of formative feedback on my work. Not every class was like that, but many were.

It was not just the class structure that changed. It was me. As I progressed through college, I gained the confidence to seek out mentors. I read and studied for personal interest, not just for a class assignment. I volunteered at a public history museum to explore my passions and interests in anthropology. I sought out peers with shared interests, and our late-night conversations far exceeded the depth that we reached in formal class settings. In other words, my education took off when I relied less on the instructor and more on my growing capacities as a person with curiosity and a love of learning.

While there is much that learning organizations can do to create higher quality learning experiences, the single most important part of an education that promotes access & opportunity is student ownership. If K-12 and higher education institutions are going to equip people to thrive as learners and throughout life, it will come from nurturing people who are not dependent upon a formal teacher-student construct. People with ownership who can self-regulate and self-direct have a huge advantage in the connected world. Where traditional literacy was once a key to the treasures of learning and opportunity, self-direction is that key in today. Resources that meet or far exceed what I experienced in a first year American civilization lecture are freely available to those who can find and take advantage of them. Empowering people to take advantage of such resources and communities is one of our best chances at making progress toward access, opportunity, even workforce development.

Beyond Students Meeting Standards

Some think about self-directed learning and wonder what place it can have in a world of increased academic standards. So much of school is becoming about helping students meet specific sets of standards in given areas. We want to know if students are proficient as defined by whether they met certain standards. This is true for our youngest learners, and it is also true in many professional programs in higher education. We want our doctors and nurses to meet set standards before they start working on and with us.

There is unquestionably a role for standards in education. We want students who are literate and who have met standards that speak to what it means to be literate. The same is true in other content areas, but it is an even higher priority when we look at certain higher education degrees in healthcare, or training programs for specific trades. Yet, meeting standards is not enough.

If part of the goal of education is to liberate, then that means creating space for people to become learners who are capable of personal growth and development regardless of whether they are in a classroom with a teacher. There are many instances where one needs to grow and develop with regard to a set of specific standards. I prefer going to a healthcare professional who at least met a minimum set of standards in medical school. I seek out an electrician with a demonstrated ability to comply with existing codes.

Of course, meeting the standards is not adequate. One of the reasons why I chose my current doctor is because she noted that she values staying current in the emerging research in medical journals. In other words, her education did not stop at medical school. She takes the initiative to continue learning and growing despite the fact that medical school is decades behind her. Similarly, I do not want an electrician who does little more than comply with the code. I want one who can face new and unique situations in my hundred-year-old house and come up with creative and safe solutions that also keep projects at a reasonable cost. The standards work fine as a baseline, but it is not enough to be a person who earned the certification or met the standards. The one who stops at the standards or certifications is the one who remains largely other-directed.

Imagine a group of teachers who stopped reading, studying, and learning when they graduated from college. They only learn what they are "forced" to do so through administratively mandated professional development days. Imagine if these teachers saw no reason to stay up on the amazing emerging research about the brain and learning. Imagine if they did not have an interest in taking the time to learn about the unique needs and interests of a new student in the class. What if they did not engage in the sort of reflective practice that allowed them to learn from their own teaching successes and failures? This group represents people who have not discovered the power and possibility of self-directed learning in helping one to pursue and sometimes achieve increasingly greater levels of excellence. From this perspective, I accept the role of standards and certifications in helping people to meet baseline skills and competencies, but we are unwise to accept them as adequate for a liberal education that prepares people to be full and active participants in a democratic society.

At the same time, I am not suggesting the standards are necessarily the best starting point. When possible, there is great power in providing people with ample space to experiment, explore, question, and drive the learning apart from pre-determined standards. Amid this learning through discovery, the people will sometimes come to a point when they need to master a certain body of knowledge to meet a goal. It is at that point when they embrace learning by standards in a new way, with a measure of purpose and intrinsic motivation.

Consider the example of learning to play baseball. To play on a team, I need to learn the rules of the game, the non-negotiables. I cannot just run to bases in random order because I feel like it, all in the name of self-direction. And yet, what should I learn first? Do we sit children down and quiz them on all the rules before they get a chance to experience parts of the game? Or, do we go to games with the kids, let them experience it, play catch with them, and give them a chance to swing at a few balls? Yes, a time will come when they will need to meet the minimum "standards" for playing the game, but that does not always need to drive the learning. There are many instances where first letting them explore and discover on their own has great benefits. Most importantly, it is a great way to tap into personal curiosity and interest, which is an incredibly powerful lever for learning.

There are exceptions to this, like teaching certain fundamental safety rules before letting someone play with a dangerous object. Even then, when time and safety considerations allow for it, leaving room for self-directed learning not only helps learners meet immediate goals, but it helps them to develop the skills and character necessary to learn future things on their own. Emerging brain research seems to support this. If we want people to engage in deep learning, then it is important to move from teacher-directed to student-directed experiences.

When asked what the recent brain research is telling us about how to teach, Dr. Matthew Peterson of the MIND Research Institute replied this way. "Stop telling them things. Have them do things, problem solve, build things, discover how things work (and don't tell them how things work)."[3] These sorts of challenges provide qualitatively different learning experiences and, over time, result in qualitatively different types of learners and people.

Simply teaching to the point of meeting set standards also has the added downside of failing to equip students who are at the

---

3. This quote comes from a session at the 2014 Education Innovation Summit in Scottsdale, Arizona.

greatest disadvantage. If schools focus upon only teaching to the standards, then the deep and self-directed learning will happen outside of the classroom, potentially more often for the students who live in environments rich with tools, safety, encouragement, and resources that help promote independence and self-direction. Without necessarily intending to do so, we have one population of students who stop at literate, while another continues on toward greater levels of fluency in a myriad of domains and skills that will help them take advantage of opportunities that remain largely unavailable to the simply literate. Self-directed learning is partly about helping people progress throughout life toward fluency, deep learning, over-learning, and the type of immersive learning that leads to deep joy, satisfactions, and excellence.

I am not pitting standards against self-directed learning. I am simply making the point that standards are usually inadequate for helping to meet the central aims of education in a democratic society. We want an education beyond standards, and a self-directed learning mindset can assist with that.

Self-Directed Learning Reality Check

You already know that I am an advocate for self-directed learning. There is no question about that. I wrote this book about it, I write about it often in other places, and I affirm its benefits so much that it has led to valid critiques that I am biting the formal education hand that feeds me. This does not mean, however, that I disregard the limitations of self-directed learning, and there are genuine potential limitations. Even as I dedicate this chapter to the reasons for self-directed learning, in a spirit of candor, I will conclude the chapter with a few limitations or reality checks.

Self-Directed Learning Reality Check 1: Opportunity

Formal credentials and degrees still open doors for people. This is true in some fields more than others. There are plenty of fields and positions where alternative pathways to demonstrating excellence are adequate for getting an interview and the job. Yet, I have witnessed dozens of situations where otherwise qualified people did not get an interview, an invitation to apply, or the job because they lacked the minimum degree qualifications on the job posting. Some people are willing to make exceptions but there are plenty of companies where people are just working at a pace and with such a volume that they rarely take the time to look for alternative evidence. Some companies only accept applicants with degrees from specific institutions. Fair or not, this is a reality. The degree is shorthand to some for being potentially qualified. It is an easy way for an initial screening. As such, there are ample situations today where not having the degree decreases your chances or sometimes restricts you from having any chance at a given job or a promotion.

As such, when write about the promise of self-directed learning, I am not arguing for it in lieu of a traditional k-12 and higher education. I offer this as what I consider an important supplement and enhancement to that education. There are many examples of self-directed learners who thrived without the formal education, and I suspect that these alternative pathways will become more commonplace in the future. Yet, we are not there, and we may never get there in some areas of study. As such, I am arguing here for a both/and approach. I see great promise in looking for ways to infuse more of this self-directed mindset and skillset into otherwise traditional learning contexts.

Self-Directed Learning Reality Check 2: Gaps

Sometimes the self-directed learning pathway leaves gaping holes in an education. A well-designed, systematic program is intended to fill most of those gaps. We can debate how well some programs do this, but certain jobs or professions call for more precision, and gaps are highly problematic. A surgeon needs to have a core set of skills and we probably do not want surgeons who have too many gaps in those core skills. This is true in other less life-or-death jobs and fields of study as well.

Of course, self-directed learners can embrace formal study and carefully constructed learning pathways that reduce gaps in learning, but not always. This is sometimes a limitation of the self-directed learning approach. Some people can learn to play an instrument independent of a teacher, but most benefit from an expert guide.

Self-Directed Learning Reality Check 3: Followership

I am quick to talk and write about developing leadership skills, but I cannot disregard the importance of learning to be a world-class follower too. Not all of us will be our own boss throughout life. Most people will hold jobs and positions where they report to others. Even when you are a CEO, you might report to a board. As such, it is important to learn to follow with excellence.

I am not sure that being a student in school is the absolute best training ground for followership. Yet, it can be a place to learn some of the associated skills of great followers, and this can be an important journey toward great leadership. There is no question that you can learn important skills of followership through a more self-directed learning experience, but I want to recognize that some of the scripted or directed aspects of a schooling experience (even in more self-directed schools) can be opportunities to learn these skills. The model that dominated much of American schooling for the decades does help many people learn how to follow.

Of course, learning followership and becoming a self-directed learner are not mutually exclusive. Learning to follow is just another learning tool for the self-directed learner. For example, when I set a goal to learn Kung Fu, I am probably not going to make as much progress if I just try to do it on my own. Part of my plan as a self-directed learner will be to find a great teacher to help me. In this way, we find that mature self-directed learners are not people who insist on doing their own way all of the time. They are just the ones who set the goals and explore the best ways to achieve the goals. Sometimes the answer is tapping into more teacher-directed environments. Yet, what is distinct is that the overall voice and choice remains with the learner.

Conclusion—The Boy Who Wanted to be a Mortician

While there are plenty of limitations and cautions for us to consider, self-directed learning plays an important role in equipping people to thrive as lifelong learners. It is a way to nurture voice. It is an opportunity to help people learn to take greater ownership. It can help address issues of access and opportunity. It can empower. It can tap into personal curiosity. It can better prepare people to achieve personally meaningful goals throughout life. It can also help people expand their sense of what is possible. To illustrate that last point, I will conclude this chapter with a story that I originally published online.[4]

When I was an undergraduate student, some others and I started an after-school tutoring program for a small group of kids in Milwaukee. It was not anything elaborate. We showed up. The kids showed up. The kids did their homework and we helped them. We ate some snacks and got a chance to get know one another.

The first young person that I worked with was a middle school boy. We mostly worked on math. He was clever, quiet, kind, and persistent. Sometimes he just needed a little extra help. For the sake of the story, I will call him Marcus.

Marcus lived with his grandmother. I never found out what happened to his parents, but I did not pry. He seemed happy living with his grandmother. He knew that she loved him and while he did not like how strict she was, he seemed to understand it. For example, the neighborhood where he lived had significant crime and drug issues, and his grandmother refused to let him play in the neighborhood. So, for Marcus, his daily schedule consisted of waking up, eating breakfast, taking the bus to school, spending the day at school, taking the bus to this tutoring program after school, getting the ride home from there, spending time in the house at

4. This last portion is a revised reprinting from a blog post that I wrote on December 21, 2016 at http://etale.org/main/2016/12/21/12731/.

night, and then starting over again the next morning. Then the big event on the weekend was spending a half day at a local Pentecostal church.

One day at tutoring, some of us were having our snacks and talking about goals. Curious, I asked Marcus what sort of goals he set for himself. Not that he needed to have everything figured out at that moment, but I asked if he had certain careers that seemed interesting to him. Marcus looked up, smiled, and proudly explained that he wanted to be a mortician. I'd never met a young man who said that his dream job was to be a mortician. This is nothing against that career. It is not typically at the top of the list for young people's potential future careers.

I do not remember how I asked it, but I inquired why. I thought perhaps he had a family member who was in that line of work, so he became familiar with it. Yet, when I asked if he had any family members or friend's family members who were morticians, he said that he did not. "Then how did you decided upon that job?" I did not know how to react to his reply. "I just thought it would be a good job," he explained, "because, in my neighborhood, I know that I'll always have work."

I wondered how many funerals Marcus attended in his life. I wondered how many friends or neighbors died. I pictured Marcus sitting in the corner of a funeral home, watching, listening, and thinking. As he saw everything happening, the tears, the grieving, the consoling, he noticed a man in a suit standing by the door, overseeing the event. The man greeted and directed people. He seemed unusually comfortable in this environment. When the event ended and Marcus left with family, he saw this man closing the casket and beginning to put things away for the night. Marcus respected this man. He was dressed well, spoke well, moved with confidence, was comfortable even when others were not, and he seemed to take pride in his role. I do not know if any of this ever happened, but it was the image that came to mind as I listened to Marcus.

So often I champion the value of getting informed about the possibilities. I write this for teachers, school leaders, policymakers and other related people; but how much more important is this for the students as well? Part of a great education is exposure and getting informed about the possibilities. This is the power of reading widely and deeply, immersive field trips, study abroad, internships, experiential education, and even just having guest speakers and visiting experts (resident artists, resident scientists, resident poets and writers, etc.). Students experience, discuss, observe, and learn.

As they are exposed to the breadth of possibilities, students also have opportunity to consider what path they might take in life. They don't need to have it all figured out at an early age, but there is a richness to learning about and appreciating the many ways in which people use their gifts, interests, and abilities to benefit themselves and others. I believe that adding more opportunities for self-directed learning can create a forum for students to explore possibilities that interest them. When done in a diverse community of learners, each student will also learn from the perspectives and experiences of others.

Maybe Marcus is a mortician today. Maybe he is an amazing mortician who does his job with excellence and has the honor of being with and assisting people at some of their most sorrowful and more challenging moments in life. Perhaps he wears a suit, is comfortable where others are not, and helps to create meaningful and memorable moments where people gather to grieve, remember, encourage, and begin the process of healing and closure. Maybe Marcus went another direction. I lost touch over the years. However, when I think about him, even today, I find myself wanting to find ways to help students experience the joy and freedom of getting informed about the possibilities. This is probably part of why I write and speak so strongly about pathways over gateways, about access and opportunity, and about self-education. To some degree, Marcus is why I wrote this book.

3

School as Resource for "Real Learning"

SELF-DIRECTED LEARNING IS A critical 21st-century skill. It is a form of literacy, the ability to learn. Alvin Tofler wrote about this when he explained that the literate of the future will be those capable of learning, unlearning, and relearning.[1] Think about the many aspects of life in a connected world: access to information, learning tools and technologies, learning to connect and communicate with people in new ways, and learning to find and make use of resources across platforms and media. Imagine the disadvantage of not knowing how to do such things in our modern world.

The digital world created massive opportunities for what some of us refer to as democratized learning. In the past, formal learning organizations controlled much of the knowledge, and acquiring that knowledge required you to go to the experts in that organization to obtain it. With the development of mass produced books, democratization of knowledge spread. People with the money to buy books obtained access to knowledge apart from school. Not all people had access to these books, however. When public libraries gained traction, even people from the poorest families gained the means to check out and learn from books across a myriad of topics, again all apart from a formal school or a teacher. Next came the Internet revolution, drastically expanding the scope of resources available to anyone. Today, if you have Internet access, you are a

1. Toffler, *Future Shock*, 414.

few clicks from books, articles, videos, mentors, communities, free courses, and so much more.

Yet, not everyone benefits from these equally. It is the self-directed learner who garners the greatest benefit, as we will discuss in greater depth when we get to the chapter on the new digital divide. The why of self-directed learning is rooted in equipping people to get the most out of this new and connected world. This has implications for many domains of life and work, but as an example, allow me to draw your attention to the workplace.

Interview leaders in companies and other organizations. Ask them what sort of skills are necessary for people to thrive and move toward growing leadership in an organization. You will get many answers, but if you find results similar to what I discovered, you will see that it takes people who are committed, people who take ownership in their work. They do not just wait for others to tell them what to do. They are not just clocking in their hours. They take initiative. They take pride in their successes and they own up to their failures. They are constantly learning and monitoring their learning, trying to get better at what they do.

Does any of this sound familiar? These are the traits of a self-directed learner. When we equip people to develop agency and ownership in their learning, we are also preparing them for agency and ownership in work and other areas of life. We are equipping them with incredible skills and attitudes that are highly sought after in the workplace. As such, a compelling why behind teaching and nurturing self-directed learners is that this is a great way to set people up for a lifetime of success in the workplace.

Of course, there are exceptions. There are some jobs that want people to be compliant, unquestioning about following the rules and procedures set by someone else. Push this button. Say exactly these phrases. Use these steps only. Then do it all over again. Yet, these are not usually jobs with security or opportunity for advancement. The jobs that give greater stability are often the ones that call upon people to think for themselves and get work done independent of constant monitoring and redirection.

As I suggested in the previous chapter, a key to access and opportunity is empowering people with a sense of agency and self-confidence. That is why this matters so much. This is why this is a critical social issue that we can tackle if we begin to empower, encourage, and create space for people to self-direct. In some ways, this is putting digital teeth on the adage: "Give the man a fish and he will have fish for a day; teach a man to fish, and he'll have fish for a lifetime." This is even more important because the fishing is truly amazing in this connected world!

The critic says that this is fine if you are an autodidact. If you are an exceptional and gifted learner, this is a wonderful concept, but it does not work for your average student. I beg to differ. In fact, I know with certainty that this works with a variety of students because I have seen it. This is something that is actually happening in our schools, whether we know it, like it, see it, or not. There are self-directed learners all around us.

Some people say something like this. Self-directed learning is great for *these* students, but not for *those* students. I suspect that there are sometimes undertones of flawed stereotypes in such statements. Too often there are beliefs that self-directed learning is for certain populations and not other populations. I am concerned about this, and I think we need to tackle it head-on because it is false. Self-directed learning and self-blended learning are visible across socioeconomic lines, across the different types of people that we have in our world and in our learning communities. We see people of all types who are capable of doing this. Some people might have backgrounds and experiences that discourage them from embracing a life of self-directed learning. Maybe they had people in their community, their family, or their schools that did not encourage them. That is a possibility, but that is not destiny. Those are not genetic predispositions away from self-directed learning. Anyone can become more self-directed over time.

I appreciate the skepticism when I mention people like Tesla, Benjamin Franklin, Thomas Edison, and Abraham Lincoln. We are not all going be a Mozart, Tesla or a Leonardo da Vinci. Yet, by learning and embracing the concepts of self-directed, we can progress toward our individual and distinct callings in life. Perhaps you started at a different place than another person in terms of your giftedness for music, art, science, or something else. Maybe it is true that you will never become the next Mozart. That does not matter. Nurtured and encouraged to embrace self-directed learning, you can get much better than you are now, and that is part of the vision. The vision is to help people start on a lifelong journey of growing competence and confidence in multiple areas.

All of this is a precursor to the main concept in this chapter, the idea of school as a resource for learning. Many of us think of school and the formal school curriculum as the primary and most important part of a person's formal learning, but this connected age challenges some of that. The democratization of learning mentioned earlier in the chapter means that learners of all ages have more than one means of learning. Sugata Mitra's well-known hole-in-the-wall experiments illustrate my point. He conducted experiments where he put computers with Internet access in walls of towns in India to see what would happen. From this, he and his colleagues describe what he calls self-organized learning environments. Without the presence of a teacher, students worked together to create meaning. They developed new literacies simply through a computer with Internet access.[2]

In such a world, schools can learn to see themselves less as keepers of knowledge and guardians of expertise. Of course, they will be places of knowledge and acquiring expertise, but they are not keepers and guardians. They can choose new metaphors. They can see themselves as launch pads of learning with the hope and assumption that student learning will extend far beyond what teachers plan for students.

With this in mind, schools can benefit from looking at themselves as resource centers. The school is one important aspect of a student's learning, even a central hub, but not the only source of learning. Teachers are not distributors of content as much as they are guides, resources, coaches, and mentors.

2. Mitra, et al., "Acquisition of Computing Literacy," 407–26.

Imagine a classroom where students arrive excited to study a topic of personal interest. Perhaps they do this self-directed learning half of the time. Then there are shared learning experiences and activities the other half of the time. Imagine a high school where each individual or small groups creates a new and driving question every quarter or semester. One student chooses to explore the causes of racism as informed by a deeply personal recent experience. Another student might want to learn about sports injuries because of a torn ligament as a dancer.

The students work with the teacher to set goals, devise a plan for exploring the question, and to select a culminating project or artifact to show what the student learned at the end of the semester. Each student will also need to present the work in a public exhibition open to the community. The dancer with the torn ligament will learn about sports medicine, human anatomy, and physical therapy. This student will also develop interviewing skills, information literacy skills, research skills, writing communication skills, time management skills, and the student will develop disciplinary literacy by working through challenging science-related texts. Beyond all of this, the student gets the experience of persisting with a project for weeks and months, something rarely done in many classrooms, but a critical skill for most leadership positions in the workplace.

The line of inquiry for each student is important, but it is also about all the learning, communication, and thinking skills developed along the way. In a learning environment like this, school is really becoming that resource for learning. The teachers are coaches and guides. The other classmates or co-learners and resources for learning as well.

This is what is happening in some schools with promising results. Of course, not every school is interested in throwing out the entire curriculum, which is why we see many hybrid approaches. While schoolwide efforts are promising, a teacher in any class or content area can gradually incorporate small elements of this approach. This can be done alongside the regular curriculum or as a more integrated and embedded part of the class. As such, there is something in this book for people across the spectrum when it comes to their views about self-directed learning. For the person who is generally content with their school and classroom, you will find plenty of ideas that you can incorporate alongside everything else that you are doing. For the person who is discontent with the system and believes that we need to rebuild from the ground up, you too will find something of value. Of course, there is something for everyone in between these two ends of the spectrum as well.

4

The Learner with a Thousand Tutors
and the Personal Learning Network

SELF-DIRECTED LEARNING IS NOT lone ranger learning. It is also not learning in isolation. Sometimes people think of it as anti-teacher, when it is actually the most pro-teacher position that you can take. When we start talking about self-directed learning, we are talking about the learner with a thousand teachers. Yet, that admittedly calls for us to redefine "teacher" so that we are able to fully understand the possibilities. Allow me to suggest this expanded, albeit a bit startling, definition of a teacher. A teacher is any experience, any person, any thing, or any group that can help you learn.

Imagine for a moment that you are a student in a class that you are excited about; it is an interesting topic. You come in, and you discover that the teacher is not interesting or engaging. The teacher is burned out, checked out, physically present, but otherwise absent from the room. What do you do as a student? Or, maybe you are in a class, and there is a well-meaning new teacher who is passionate about the topic but can only take you so far. You are deeply curious and have questions that go beyond the boundaries of the class and maybe that teacher's expertise. Or, perhaps you have one of these passions or interests that is not part of the formal curriculum. It gets mentioned but nothing more. Teachers usually have a focus. They have certain material that they want or need to cover and certain objectives they need to focus upon. That is just how school works much of the time.

Yet, self-blended learners have access to a world of teachers and tutors. Everything around them is a teacher. Every person around them is a teacher. What does it mean to take advantage of these thousand tutors that you have available to you? Let me suggest suggest a couple of ideas

Conduct an inventory of your own life. Think back about your childhood up to the modern day. Create a list of all of the people who helped you learn something. Do not limit it to the people with the formal title of teacher or professor. Just make a list of people who helped you learn. If you want, you can stretch yourself to think about the other teachers in your life, not just people, but groups, experiences, formative books, and other resources that served as teachers and guides for you along the way. Commit to creating this list for ten to fifteen minutes. I encourage you to actually do this. Set this book aside and write out your list. Then we can continue.

You likely have an impressive list, the vast majority of whom are not formal teachers. You are well on your way to revealing the fact that you are already a learner with a thousand tutors. Why not make this a more central and recognized part of each student's formal learning as well? Why not help them recognize their list of tutors and grow that list? Why not help them tap into the people on that list to achieve their learning goals now and well into the future? This is not only an asset for their present learning, but it is helping them build a lifelong network, something that we will examine more broadly in an upcoming chapter.

Now try this exercise. Think about something that you love to learn, something for which you have a deep passion and interest. Now devote five to ten minutes searching the web for people and resources related to that topic. Create a list of interesting discoveries. If you could learn about these things from anyone or anything in the world, what would it be? Maybe you could do a search for the top ten most knowledgeable or skilled people in the world on the subject. Or, you could search for the best resources in the world. Just look around for them, and build this list. If you want to be courageous, try the third step. Reach out to some of those people. Tell them about your interests. Tell them about what you know and what you do not know. Share a few questions with them. Maybe ask if they would be willing to connect with you in a Google Hangout or some kind of live chat. Or you can ask if they are willing to interact with you via email. I think you will be surprised to find what happens. There are many people who love being teachers. The thing is, people who have become experts in areas usually want to share that expertise with others. They have a passion for it, and it is difficult for them to contain. They want to let it out, and they do. You can be a recipient of that.

The Personal Learning Network

Now we can expand on this idea by looking at a concept that is likely familiar to many readers, the personal learning network. There are countless articles and several books on personal learning networks for students, but I am going to suggest that we expand this to think about students, building off the idea of a learner with a thousand tutors. As I help teachers in traditional schools explore ways to integrate self-directed learning into their otherwise conventional curriculum and classrooms, I consistently find that the student personal learning network is one of the easiest but most impactful approaches.

Personal Learning Networks have been around for some time. The idea of a PLN is simply a network of people and resources through which you learn and grow. Books like *Personal Learning Networks: Using the Power of Connections to Transform Education*[1] and *The Connected Educator: Learning and Leading in a Digital Age*[2] both give a helpful introduction to this concept and what it means for educators.

1. Richardson and Mancabelli. *Personal Learning Networks.*
2. Nussbaum-Beach and Hall. *The Connected Educator.*

However, there is a smaller and potentially even more significant conversation about personal learning networks that is taking place. That consists of a growing number of us who are looking at the idea of a personal learning network, combining it with the promise and possibility of self-directed learning, and starting to think more about how we might empower and encourage students to cultivate their own personal learning networks.

What if learning communities and organizations made student personal learning networks an integral part of the learning experience? As students progress through their schooling years, what if they cultivated a deeper and more substantive global personal learning network?

Informed by the idea of connectivism, a student personal learning network is one that helps students not only learn about a given topic, but also grow in their understanding of how to cultivate and make use of knowledge networks. It is one thing to study world geography out of a textbook. It an entirely different experience to connect with people around the world, learning from each, comparing and contrasting geography in different parts of the world, and building meaningful and sometimes persistent connections with those people.

A Little Learning Theory Background

If we examine some of the trends in education over the past century, we can see them as extensions of four learning theories: behaviorism, cognitivism, constructivism, and connectivism. Behaviorism is where we get things like measurable learning objectives in education. This is the body of work focused upon observable behavior, rewards, punishments, classical conditioning, and operant conditioning. Behaviorism is often associated with names like Watson, Skinner, and Thorndike.

The influence of behaviorism in education can be traced to the early part of the 20th century, but it continues to inform thought and practice today.[3] It informed the work of many scholars and educators over the last century, and it can also be seen as a significant influence in the push toward the use of observable and measurable learning objectives. Teachers in the 1960s and 1970s were introduced to this idea through books like Robert Mager's *Preparing Instructional Objectives*[4], but by the 1980s use of such objectives became common practice in schools around the United States. If you cannot see it, measure it, or document it, then it loses significance from a behaviorist's perspective.

Alongside the influence of behaviorism we saw the development of cognitivism. One of the more well-known educational influences of this movement relates to the idea of developmental psychology, when we discovered that the brain develops in certain stages and we can start to plan learning experiences based upon where people are in these developmental stages. Where behaviorism focused upon external observable behavior, cognitivism invited attention to the inner workings of brain.

Constructivism emerged amid these two perspectives on learning, adding yet another strand to the conversation. As the name might suggest, constructivism focused upon the idea that knowledge is not simply something that one person transfers to another, but knowledge is constructed within an individual through experience. For many educators, John Dewey is likely the first name that comes to mind when thinking about such ideas. You may also think of people like Vygotsky, Kolb, and Montessori.

While I represent these three learning theories as if they came in a nice and neat chronology, the reality is that they often crossed paths with another. We see ample evidence of them intermingling, especially when we look at educational models and practices over the last century. Today it is common to find educators who describe their educational philosophy and practice in a way that seems to relate to all three of these in one way or another.

More recently, even into the 21st century, we find yet another perspective added to the conversation. George Siemens

3. Staddon, *The New Behaviorism*.

4. Mager, *Preparing Instructional Objectives*.

introduced connectivism, which seems to suggest that knowledge is not simply something that exists in our brains.[5] Instead, knowledge exists in our connections with other people, resources and communities. This resonates with the experience of many in this digital and information age, as we often find that our connections with others is what enables us to work and flourish. Medical professionals rely upon complex data systems and other professionals for certain tasks. Even historians, sometimes thought of as solitary scholars, now share rich data sets on the web and collaborate with one another to carry out research goals and tasks.[6]

Self-directed Learning Revisited

Now we can turn our attention back to the topic of self-directed learning for a moment. As I look at learning organizations today, I see two major approaches to teaching and learning. I will use a fishing analogy that I alluded to earlier in the text for this example. Some schools are set up as fish distribution centers. They are like fish markets where a person is given a fish and can then prepare it and eat it. Other learning organizations function more like places of fishing lessons. They do not just give out the fish. They teach the people how to fish for themselves. The first is the school that seems content with distribution as the goal, leaving the learners dependent upon a teacher to grow and learn. The second focuses upon equipping learners with the ability to learn for themselves, allowing them to develop the skills necessary to thrive as learners for life. From this perspective, the goal of a learning organization is to help students progress toward independence.

In reality, few learning organization are one or the other of these two. They are most often at some point in a spectrum between the two. Some focus upon content distribution with some opportunity for self-directed learning, while others are heavy on self-directed learning with occasional content distribution. An

5. Siemens, "Connectivism."

6. See the Trans-Atlantic Slave Trade Database as an example, http://slavevoyages.org/.

easy way to think about this is to consider the spectrum of a school based upon four questions that we examined in the first chapters of this book. On the one side we have a more teacher-directed approach. On the right side, we have a more self-directed approach. Usually we find schools that vary on the spectrum for the four questions. Whatever the case, my argument is that our goal is for all learners to eventually be empowered and able to function on the far right side of this chart.

Pulling it All Together

This finally brings us back to idea of a student personal learning network, which is a mix of connectivism and self-directed learning. As defined at Wikipedia, "A personal learning network is an informal learning network that consists of people a learner interacts with and derives knowledge from . . . "[7] When I ask people to describe their personal learning network, they sometimes start by listing the technologies that they use, tools like Twitter, blogs, YouTube, and various communication tools. That is understandable because these are the tools that allow them to connect with their network. However, I argue that the network is largely the people, communities and resources; not the technologies themselves. If I showed you a picture of a large public swimming pool full of people and asked you to describe what you saw, you would likely not describe the technology of a swimming pool. You would instead talk about the people, what they were doing, and how they are behaving. Similarly, a personal learning network is first about our relationships and connections with people and resources, hence the idea of a learner with a thousand tutors. We use the tools to strengthen, lengthen, and make such connections.

7. Personal Learning Network, https://en.wikipedia.org/wiki/Personal_learning_network.

A Student Personal Learning Network

A student personal learning network is, therefore, a rich and ever-growing series of connections with people, resources, and communities around the world, connections that allow learners to grow in knowledge, skill, ability, and perspective. What if we spent more time thinking about the networks that students are building as they go through their schooling years? What are the tools and technologies that they use and how are they using them? One of many connections in this network will likely be one or more teachers. It will also include classmates, family members, community members, and others with whom they learn and interact in the physical world. As it expands over the years, it will also include people far beyond the walls of the home, school and community.

What if we made it part of the curriculum for students to build such a network, inviting students to keep a log or journal of their growing network, and how this network is empowering them to learn. How is it expanding their knowledge and perspective? How are they building a meaningful network? This would genuinely turn schools into places of fishing lessons. Students can interview people around the world, tutor, and be tutored. They can take part in formal and informal learning communities. They can participate in Twitter chats and Hangouts, learn from and engage in the blogosphere the world of podcasts. They can experience the power of working on a meaningful project in a distributed or virtual team. They can participate in a massive open online course (or design and teach one). They can share resources through social bookmarking and other technologies, host and take part in webinars, and build new online and blended learning communities around topics of personal value, need, and interest.

Over time, the students will not only build a personal learning network. They will also venture into starting their own personal teaching networks, being agents of change and positive influence in the digital world and beyond. This is a learning exercise that can extend across courses and grades. Of course, their network goes with them after they graduate as well.

Practical First Steps

There are four simple steps to get started with this.

1. Introduce students to the idea of a personal learning network and have them create a map of that network using their favorite mind-mapping tool. If you have one, share your PLN as an example. Be sure to spend time on the "why" of a PLN. Then invite students to add to and refine this network over the year.

2. Set aside time for PLN show and tell. This is a time where students display the visual of their network to others, describing how they use it and how it helps them. On occasion, have students explain what is new in their network, how it was added, and how it helps them. This provides a wonderful opportunity for peer-to-peer learning.

3. Create simple challenges where learners find a problem, try to solve it, and periodically report back to the group. They will build and leverage their network to solve the problems. Along the way, they will not only find potential solutions, but they will experience the power of connected learning.

4. If you are working with younger students, consider building a class PLN, where you map it out on the wall, and you collectively add to it throughout the year through Skype sessions, Google Hangouts and other connections with people and groups around the world. When you face a new challenge as a class, ask the students, "Is there anything in our PLN that could help us with this? Do we need to expend or expand our PLN in some way?"

Networked Learning

In *Informal Learning*, Jay Cross describes the changing nature of human organizations, business, computers, and learning in the 21st century. Referencing the work of Tom Malone (MIT), Cross explains that networks consistently evolve in three stages. The first is disconnected nodes or what he calls bands. Think of the days where there was the butcher shop, the blacksmith, the carpenter, the baker, and others in a single town. Each one represented a distinct and separate band. The second is a more hierarchical model which he calls kingdoms. Now think of a company that owns and operates the bakery, mill, butcher shop, and the other entities that were previously independent. They report up through what we think of as an organizational chart. The last is a largely organic and interconnected set of nodes, which he calls democracy. There is no obvious leader, but they are connected with one another in many ways, collaborating as needed. Cross uses these to explain how human organizations go through these same three stages as they move to a networked society. It is the same for business operations and even learning within an organization (the focus of Cross's book).[8]

This is a brilliant illustration because I can overlay it on a dozen different communities and organizations with which I work, and it provides rich insights about what is working, what is not, why there are seeming conflicts, why things sometimes just "click," and why some of us just seem to be talking right past each other. We are living and thinking about different stages. A typical University, for example, might have faculty functioning as independent nodes, administration function in the hierarchy, and students thinking and function more in that democratic stage. You can imagine how this can and does cause tension. This is a powerful tool for explaining the communication breakdowns and conflicting values in learning communities.

Allow me to illustrate from a formal schooling setting. In the K-12 world, there is the community, the school board, the superintendent, the principal, department chairs, classroom teachers, and students. For many, they are thinking of this from a stage two perspective. This is a hierarchy. Where do parents fit into the picture? They are part of the community, but I wonder if this is not part of why I consistently see tensions about the role of parents. If parents stay out of the way or just play the role of helping their kids fit into the hierarchy, all is well (from some people's perspective).

8. Cross, *Informal Learning*, 6–7.

If, on the other hand, parents are communicating messages to kids that do not align with what the teachers want, or the parents want to influence what happens in the school, then there are problems.

Or, what if a student chooses to learn about things outside of school, by using separate tutors, through self-study, or something else? We have another potential conflict. The teachers thinking from a stage two perspective may well see this as a challenge to their authority and rightful place in the hierarchy. All works well as long as the students do things the teacher's way, according to the teacher's timing and standard.

As Cross explains in his text, people in different stages have different ways of thinking. He describes the traits of people thinking at stage two versus stage three thinking. Stage three thinking is organic, seemingly chaotic at times, and participatory. People are multifaceted, the organization is emergent, cooperation trumps competition, and change is constant and welcome. For a stage two organization, things are carefully managed, linear, controlled, predictable, deliberately designed, competitive, and change is a concern.[9]

The more I think about this comparison, the more I suspect that part of the struggle and growing pains experienced by many people and learning organizations today comes from the fact that we have the clash of stage two and three thinking.

I participate in many online communities ranging from Twitter chats to private professional networks, communities of practice to MOOCs. I approach most of them from a stage three mindset. I recognize that there might be a formal leader, but I find myself frustrated when that leader seeks to control too much. I have seen such a mindset stifle the energy and passion of many online groups. These hierarchical thinking leaders are running it like a stage two community, and while I can appreciate lessons and experiences from such organizations, I thrive on the messiness and inter-connectivity of stage three contexts.

There are still authorities, leaders, and people with different degrees of influence in stage three communities, but some still function from the mindset that you need one central leader or

9. Cross, 10.

coordinator who functions almost like a puppet master. That may or may not be true for various communities and efforts, but the presence of a leader does not need to conflict with stage three thinking. They can work together. It just takes a leader with humility who does not need everything to be closely managed by a single person.

It calls for a leader who persistently welcomes people to step up and take things in unexpected directions, to network and collaborate in wonderful ways.

Communication is another clash between stage two and three thinking. A stage two leader might scold learners for talking to too many different people, advising them to focus on their assigned tasks and not others. What might be happening, however, is that the one person is doing stage three thinking: networking, collaborating across teams, exploring topics from different angles, seeing a broader perspective and deeper insights that inform their work. Trying to force stage three thinkers into a stage two world is likely to frustrate, and it might cause organizations to lose some of their best talent.

On the flip side, there are stage three thinkers who are crossing traditional boundaries, improvising, and diving into the chaos; but they have missed a critical part of the stage three context. The nodes are inter-connected. In a stage two organization, if I do something differently, the communication structure is more carefully controlled. In a stage three organization, the person making a change often needs to communicate much more broadly, developing a nuanced understanding of all the different people impacted by a decision. This is where we get the messiness. I need to be thinking about the thirty people impacted by a decision and communicate to them. I need to have a means by which they become aware of what is happening. They need to be able to give me feedback that might lead to a changed direction. Stage two thinkers are likely to be frustrated with all this "over-communication" and they may also work from more of a "need to know mindset," being careful not to "bother" subordinates with information that the leader deems unnecessary for them. These two habits of thought clash because different strategies work on one stage and not another.

Left unaddressed, this leaves people frustrated with themselves, the organization, and/or others in the organization.

We have people with strong convictions about how the organization or classroom should operate. People have preferences for a stage one, stage two, or stage three way of thinking. People may not even realize that they are battling over these differences because a certain way of thinking may be all they have ever known. As such, one step toward a resolution seems to be surfacing the source of the challenge.

What about learning in the digital age? How does all of this stage one, two, and three talk relate to nurturing self-directed learners in a school or classroom? Some people approach their learning from a stage two way of thinking. They await direction from a leader to shape their learning. Tell me what to learn and how to learn it. Yet, those same people may also operate from a stage three mindset for learning when they are away from school or the workplace. They choose what, how, and when to learn about gardening, playing an instrument, discovering the nuances of having a new house built, finding the best prices for a product or service, etc. It seems to me that we think differently about learning depending upon the context.

The problem is that a person with stage two thinking in the classroom is likely to experience a limit to their growth in an organization. They follow rules well, but they never learned to own their learning and to improvise. They wait for orders. When told what and how to learn, they do it well. What happens when they encounter problems with unclear solutions? They turn to an authority to solve it for them or they are overwhelmed. This is more than just collaborating with their boss and others to explore a solution (which seems valuable and wise). They want someone to direct them. Just tell me what to do.

I see this tension between stage two and three thinking in some of our schools, and I am concerned about it. I read student complaints about professors, and parent complaints about K-12 teachers who did not give students the answers. "How am I supposed to learn something if they don't give me the answers?"

There are teachers who think the same way. They are wonderfully organized, often engaging and beloved; but they are not necessarily helping students develop into stage three learners. We have schools that are re-imagining formal education with stage three thinking in mind, and there is much that we can learn from these schools. I have learned about and visited dozens of these schools, and I've learned that it can be approached effectively in different ways. In fact, every stage three school is unique. We can learn from them, but there is no certain recipe for perfectly replicating them (a difference between a sentient living organism and a machine).

It is still important to be able to learn from highly structured and authoritarian contexts. That is a valuable life skill even in an increasingly connected world. I turn to "experts" all the time to sit at their feet and learn from them. I can enjoy a good lecture or keynote. I appreciate the fact that I do not know what I do not know, and that I sometimes need to trust or lean on those ahead of me to get a solid start when learning something new or complex. This is important, but it just is not enough today.

It is why I often refer back to the value of helping students build their personal learning networks. When I interview people, I always ask them what they do to stay current in their work, how they spend unstructured time on the job. I ask how they go about learning something new and how they seek to solve messy problems. I ask how they function in contexts with the goals are unclear, and what they would do if suddenly said that everything on their "to-do list" at work was complete. When I hire someone, I am looking for self-directed learners, and helping one cultivate such thinking and habits is a wonderful gift that will better prepare students for life and learning in an increasingly networked global society. If we fail to help students become confident and competent with level three thinking, we may be unknowingly setting them up for disappointment and frustration in the workplace and as lifelong learners. If we recognize the reality of these two ways of thinking, we have an exciting opportunity to help ourselves and others learn to thrive in a world where stage two and stage three thinking are frequently conflicting and interacting with one another.

5

The Digital Divide

EVERY STUDENT MATTERS, BUT not evert student is set up for success. That first sentence is the essence of why the concept of the
digital divide matters today. While some people argue that the
problem of the digital divide is exaggerated, I will leave that for
you to decide. To provide some context, consider the following the
categories of digital divide.

Three Categories of the Digital Divide

We often segment the digital divide into three distinct but related
categories: hardware access, Internet access, and cognitive tools.
The first one is the conversation about the digital divide in terms of
hardware and software, the haves and the have-nots. If you have a
computer, you can take advantage of what a computer can do. If you
do not, then you find yourself missing promising opportunities.

When I was less than twelve years old, my father bought me a
computer for Christmas. After opening it, my father looked at me
and told me to learn how to use this computer because it was the
future. That was in the early 1980s and it is hard to argue with his
prediction. Computers are everywhere and computer literacy is a
basic and expected set of proficiencies. Imagine the limitations in
life if you do not know how to write and edit a paper on a computer, how to load and use software, how to save and transfer files,

and other tasks that are common and expected aspects of life. Of course, this is no longer adequate.

A solitary computer is useful, but the greatest power comes when it is connected to the rest of the world, which is the second category of the digital divide, which is focused upon broadband Internet access. This connects you to more people, news, and resources than any other time in history. During President Obama's second term, there was a time when he advocated funding for the Internet in the homes of low-income families. Why in the world would we spend money on giving people Internet access? Since when did cat videos and Facebook become access and opportunity issues? What about food, jobs, and other more fundamental needs? That was the reaction of the critics.

The reason behind this push was the digital divide. In a world where more of the resources are going online, not having immediate access is an increasingly larger disadvantage. Some job postings are only online today, not to mention their preference on how you apply. If you have limited or no Internet access, then you are missing out on job opportunities, the most current and diverse news sources, learning resources, the ability to connect as broadly and readily with experts around the world, consumer resources, and more. This might seem small or insignificant, but not having access unquestionably puts people at a disadvantage.

Internet access is not just about getting news and resources; it is also about sharing and connecting with others. This is the idea behind Austin Kleon's little book *Show Your Work*.[1] In his text, Kleon proposes that not being online and not sharing your own work online makes you largely invisible to much of the modern world. The Internet is where we make countless connections with people and resources, and not being there limits those connections. I experience this on a daily basis as I share my early and rough draft writing ideas online to garner feedback, promote conversations, and build connections. In doing so, I learn from and connect with people throughout the world, not to mention people who live right next to me but first learn about my work online.

1. Kleon, *Show Your Work!*

Some argue that this is great in an ideal world, but it is not how most people make use of the Internet. I agree. Many people limit their usage to entertainment, shopping, and connecting with friends on social media. At the same time, there many others who are harnessing the power of the Internet for learning and connections, and people gain many advantages and benefits from this. I contend that this is a valuable life skill for our age.

Maybe you have the Internet but you are going to a school that does not teach you how take advantage of it or how to use it for learning and achieving personal goals. We know that some learning happens when students have more free and unstructured time to explore and hang out online. This might come in the form of nurturing a hobby, something ranging from computer programming to fan fiction, learning a foreign language to finding a tutorial on how to play an instrument. This less directed time is, some suggest, an increasingly important way of learning today. As such, there is concern about the divide between students with access for this free exploration and those who do not have access. Guidance at schools is valuable, especially in helping some students discover the learning power of the web, but access in free time is useful for that more self-directed time. Or, we can begin to imagine ways to provide some of that free and exploration time as part of the school experience.

Then there is a third phase of the digital divide, but this is largely internal, psychological. It is the divide between one person who says, "I can" and the other person who says, "I can't." It is about the psychological tools that you develop, ones that will help more than hinder your learning and progress. Once you have Internet access and the hardware, I argue that this is one of the most important aspects of the digital divide. What about those internal barriers that are keeping people from thriving and taking advantage of life in this new connected world? This is where self-directed learning returns as an important aspect of the modern learning environment. There is a divide between those who are competent and confident as self-directed learners and those who are not.

A 2014 study suggested that people who graduate high school with higher Grade Point Averages and with the higher test scores are more likely to have higher incomes, and their quality of life is supposed to be better as well (at least, their sense of well-being in their life).[2] It is an interesting study, leading some to conclude that the key to opportunity is getting student GPAs as high as possible. If we do that, then the problem is solved.

I am not convinced that is going to solve the problem, and even if it does, it will cause new problems. Let me give you an example of something that challenges this grade point average concept. Imagine that two people graduate from the same college, with the same degree, with the same GPA, they are both interested in the same job, and they apply for it. They both go through the application process, and one graduate is clearly ahead of the other in the eyes of the interviewers. The company hires the one and not the other. Let us say that other graduate perseveres and moves on, applying for five more jobs, but does not get hired. This is a realistic scenario. We can find examples of it, which suggests that GPA and test scores do not tell the entire story. We all know that GPA is not the only factor, but what is the entire story?

There are other traits that are important for us in our lives, in our lives as citizens, in our families, in the workplace, and beyond. Helping people recognize the importance of these other skills and nurturing them is a key to empowering self-directed learners. Some people actually suggest that bringing character traits and mindsets into the conversation is classist, that we do not tell the wealthy and elite families that they need to develop these skills. I am not convinced that is true. In fact, we can find people from all classes and all socioeconomic statuses who have these other skills that are not represented as clearly through GPA and test scores. I am referring to a long list of traits like grit and perseverance, learning the power of certain forms of practice over others, conscientiousness, the ability to postpone gratification, problem-solving, collaboration, goal-setting, social skills, emotional intelligence, and many more.

2. French, Homer, Popovici, and Robins, "What You Do in High School Matters," 370–86.

These are all traits that we can nurture by creating more opportunity for self-directed learning. At the 2015 SXSWEdu Conference in Austin Text, I attended a session by a representative of Koru. The representative described their work on college graduate readiness, especially those who graduate from a great school, with a great GPA, but according to employers, they are missing something else. Koru tried to codify this and narrow it down to seven areas. They call it the Koru 7. They include grit, rigor, polish, impact, curiosity, teamwork, and ownership.[3]

According to their research, these are the traits that help people thrive in the workplace, but if you think about it, they are traits that work well in family, in citizenship, in the workplace, in community—all over the place. Proponents of the liberal arts might look at a list like that and argue that a quality liberal arts college degree is an excellent way to nurture such traits, but at least in the case of Koru's research, that is not necessarily happening.

Part of the challenge comes back to nurturing a mindset of self-directed learning. Consider how the Koru 7 shows up as students work on more self-directed learning and projects in a school. They learn grit as they preserve with a problem, project, or question over weeks and months, not just for a single unit or lesson. They do not just finish an assignment and move on to the next one. They need to dig deep, stretching and challenging their abilities (rigor). They must persist until they have a refined and elegant answer or solution, and they are able to communicate it effectively to others (polish). They learn to ask questions, explore, and experiment (curiosity). Along the way, they work with others to accomplish shared goals, assist classmates, and gain needed assistance from people in and out of the classroom (teamwork and collaboration). They must take the lead on all of this and see it through to the end (ownership). Of course, depending upon the nature of their project, they also have opportunity to engage in work that makes a difference and has a demonstrable and lasting benefit (impact).

3. For more information about Koru, visit their website at: http://www.joinkoru.com/koru-7/.

These are traits that help us grow as competent and confident self-directed learners. If you visit schools and classrooms, you will find countless teachers who believe in these traits, but the curricula and learning experiences are not designed to intentionally, strategically nurture them. Some schools are adjusting, but others are not. Nurturing these kinds of capacities in every learner will help overcome that digital divide more than anything else. The starting point is simple. We start by asking an important pair of questions. How can we nurture these non-cognitive skills that are just as important as measures like grade point average and test score? Why types of learning experiences and learning environments will best foster the development of these skills? As more teachers and schools deeply and honestly grapple with these questions, they find that some of our traditional practices are holding us back from achieving these important goals. They soon start to seek out and implement new strategies that quite often end up looking more like self-directed learning.

A Fourth Category

While hardware and software, Internet access, and mental tools are usually the three main areas of digital divide that we discuss, I want to finish this chapter with one that warrants being set apart as a fourth and distinct category. This is about access to possibilities and perspectives that nurture a sense of purpose and meaning making for students. It is not unlike what I described earlier in the book when I told the story about the boy who wanted to be a mortician when he grew up.

In northern Wisconsin there are not a lot of people. I visit there a few times and year and you can easily find spots where you see more wildlife than people. Imagine a young woman who lives in North Wisconsin. She lives in a small town of one hundred, and she has Internet access. She reads a book through the library that captured her interest. It was about some of the endangered species in the world. Maybe it was about saving endangered whales.

Since there are not many whales in North Wisconsin, I doubt that you will find many activists focused on saving the whales. This young woman is not going find a local group or community to nurture this passion, but when it comes to the digital world, the connected world, she can. She has the ability to get online and find other people who are passionate about this topic. By building such connections with people online, she is also igniting a passion in herself. She is developing and growing this interest in a topic that could make a difference in her life, and maybe eventually, as she gets older, she will have the opportunity to travel. This could take her on a completely different direction in life, and it all started with some curiosity from a book that led her online, and connected her to people in groups that she would have never met in person. She did not come from a family that traveled widely, so the Internet was probably one of her online outlets for making this type of a connection.

Notice the learning that took place in the story that I just outlined. This young woman explored something initially unfamiliar to her. She found content online about the subject. She connected with others personally engaged with and informed about the subject. From there she expanded her knowledge and even developed a set of values and convictions about it. She was a self-directed learner, not inhibited by the digital divide.

6

Common Barriers to Self-blending

IF YOU ARE STILL reading, then you likely agree with me that self-directed learning has promising possibilities. Perhaps you already suspected that when you picked up the book. Self-directed learning is a powerful way of equipping people to thrive and survive in this connected world, but there are also common challenges and barriers to moving in this direction. These challenges and barriers are not impossible to overcome, but it will take time, persistence, and commitment. It also helps to know about these challenge before experiencing them in your classroom and school. That is the purpose of this chapter. I will outline a short list of common challenges and barriers while also offering a few insights on how to work through them. These insights come from my direct experiences, as well as my study and observation of self-directed learning efforts in a variety of learning communities.[1]

Over the past decade, I began to incorporate more self-directed learning opportunities within otherwise traditional courses. These typically took different forms of project-based learning,

1. Please note that some of the ideas in this chapter, as in other parts of this text, first appeared on my blog, Etale.org. I use that as a place to test and refine my ideas. Based upon feedback from readers, I sometimes develop them into elements of a text like this one. In this particular chapter, one portion is drived from a previously published article called, "Overcoming Challenges in the Move Toward Self-Directed Learning," http://etale.org/main/2013/12/02/overcoming-challenges-in-the-move-toward-self-directed-learning/.

with learners having different levels of self-direction. Most of these courses took place in otherwise traditional learning organizations with learners who are deeply rooted in traditional ideas about school. From these direct experiences, observing self-directed learning efforts in other classrooms, and interviewing people who are working through the process of implementing more opportunities for self-directed learning, certain common reactions begin to emerge. These reactions range from those who are delighted with the opportunity and thrive, to those who consider such practices an abdication of the proper role as teacher. Let us examine some of these reactions more closely.

The Schooling Discourse

Especially when working with future and current teachers, these are typically people who accept (or at least tolerate) the traditional idea of schooling and related constructs. While some dislike them, most are comfortable thinking about learning in terms of letter grades, quizzes, tests, homework, lesson plans, credit hours, grade point averages, learning objectives, discrete courses and subjects, standards, the role of student, and the role of teacher. While those of us involved with other forms of learning are well aware that none of these are necessary for high-impact learning, such terms constitute the dominant discourse in formal education. There are certainly different opinions about each of these terms or phrases and how we use them, but there is a common acceptance that they make up the vocabulary of an educator. I mention this because each of these terms conjure certain memories and expectations about a formal learning experience. More broadly, this means that efforts in self-directed learning sometimes clash with certain traditional notions of formal schooling. As a result, those who value or find comfort in such constructs may become resistant or critical of alternatives.

There are two main ways to approach this challenge: build on new ground, or re-describe and expand on existing terms. One is to focus upon new ground, learning experiences outside of the confines of traditional schooling. People do not expect to use "schooling" terminology when they are exploring a topic for fun and on their "free time." Most of us do not use schooling vocabulary when we think of relationships, hobbies, or even our work. The digital world gives us ample opportunities to do this, with the rapid growth in resources for informal and self-directed learning on the web. A second option is to expand on the definitions of schooling terms, to engage in re-description of these terms. This involves accepting the value of a term like assessment, but then expanding our understanding of assessment by discussing concepts like assessment as learning, self-assessment, and peer-to-peer learning. In my work, this second option seems to provide the most value since the learners that I serve are usually in more traditional schooling settings. At the same time, a few high-impact experiences with the first approach (out-of-school learning) is a powerful tool for helping us consider the possibilities. Debriefing those experiences with discussion about what we can apply to our schools has great potential.

While the Brain Thrives on Novelty, it also Find Comfort in Familiarity

Even while some people are open to exploring new approaches to teaching and learning, too rapid of a shift toward self-directed learning can provoke fear, self-doubt, criticism, and uncertainty. As a result, introducing self-directed learning is often not effective with an overnight transformation of the classroom. Many will not be prepared emotionally or intellectually for such a task.

As you will read more than once in this book, a simple way of thinking about teacher-directed versus self-directed is by looking at the questions that drive the design of a lesson or unit: What do students need to learn? How will I know if they learned it? How will I monitor their progress? How will I help them learn it? The goal of self-directed learning is to eventually turn each of those into student-centered questions: What do I need to learn? How will I know when I have learned it? How will I monitor my progress?

How will I learn it? If learners lack the competence, confidence or both of these to ask and answer such questions, that will conjure negative emotions and reactions.

The good news is that many students and teachers are used to these types of questions. That is why I will later outline how we can use this familiar vocabulary to invite the students into designing some of their learning experiences or at least part of an existing learning experience. We can use the familiarity of these terms to alleviate some anxiety while gradually shifting the locus of control from teacher to student.

Self-directed Learning Skills

One of the more effective ways to address this lack of competence or confidence is to devise a plan to help students grow in their capacity to ask and answer the questions of the self-directed learner. We can do this gradually, starting by inviting learner input on the goals for a given unit and how to best assess the learning. There may be "non-negotiable" standards or outcomes, but learners can enhance or supplement them. They can also cooperate with the teacher to create a solid assessment plan. In addition, self-directed learning can be preceded by formal opportunities to grow in skills with goal-setting, self-assessment methods and strategies, skills in self-monitoring, and building a toolbox of learning and self-teaching strategies. Many teachers find great success by actually devoting interactive lessons on these discrete skills so that students can develop the competence to self-direct more fully.

This is not unlike teaching someone to drive. At first they learn about driving in a driver's education class. Then they get to practice driving but with closer supervision. Later they might get a probationary driver's license that allows them to drive with an appropriate and licensed adult. Finally, once they pass the written and driving test, they earn a license to drive on their own. I am not necessarily suggesting that we replicate that exact process, but some sort of scaffolded effort to prepare students for this level of independence and give the student, teacher, parents, and others time to understand and prepare for later and more immersive self-directed learning opportunities. In fact, even in schools that are almost entirely designed around self-directed learning, it is common for them to have one resource course or extended learning experience that helps prepare students with some of the key skills for thriving as a self-directed learner.

When I have incorporated opportunity for self-directed learning in classes, the struggles usually relate to this area of competency and/or confidence. Some students are able to flourish right away, while others seek more direction and guidance. From my perspective, this is natural, and it speaks to the ongoing value of a teacher/mentor/coach for groups of learners, helping each learner progress toward greater levels of independence. Necessary support, mentoring and resources often make the differences between a successful and unsuccessful move toward self-directed learning.

Missing the "Why" of Self-Directed Learning

We dedicated an entire chapter to this subject, but skills and confidence are not the online factor, and a compelling reason for self-directed learning is helpful for all stakeholders. Beliefs and values play a critical role. For this reason, the why of self-directed learning is a critical conversation. It is not adequate to talk about it once and then move on. This needs to be a frequent, maybe even daily conversation, especially at the beginning.

In fact, for it to be successful, this requires a cultural change within learning organizations, a move toward a compelling why. Why self-directed learning? What is limiting about the traditional teacher-directed environment? This challenges us to look at the broader aims of education. This is where we might look at self-directed learning as a means of championing human agency, increasing access and opportunity, and the critical import of self-efficacy to address any number of broader issues in society. We can also ground it in how the skills of self-directed learning with empower and equip learners to more fully achieve their current and future goals. This comes through discussion, storytelling, real world examples, and a guided activities that give ample opportunity for self-discovery of the many compelling reasons behind self-directed learning. You know that you are making progress in this area when the students and parents start to effectively and passionately articulate the important reasons behind the shift.

Teacher Convictions and Values

Teachers do not usually go into the profession because of the size of the paycheck. They obviously need a living wage, but most teachers go into education because they care about students, what they will teach, or maybe a combination of the three. Yet, even before becoming a classroom teacher, we develop a set of beliefs and convictions about what works and what does not work in education. We have our preferred practices, methods, and approaches. Sometimes we refine these convictions based upon research and careful consideration, but not always. Sometimes our idea emerge from personal experiences both as students and teachers.

These convictions are evident in almost every classroom. Just ask a group of teachers to tell you about what they do in their classrooms, and they will quickly start to incorporate some of their convictions and their values.

"In my class, every student matters."

"In my classroom, students are kind, courteous, quiet, and organized."

"My classroom is fun and playful, but everyone knows that I'm the boss."

"In my class, everyone works hard. That is a non-negotiable. When you step in the room, you are ready to work."

"I like to keep a tight rein on the class so we stay focused."

"There is a time and place for everything in my classroom."

Each of these statements not only represent what happens a teacher's classroom. They also give us clues about the teacher's underlying beliefs and values. This is an important starting place because a common barrier for self-directed learning relates to teacher beliefs and values. In my experience, there are three main challenges that in this regard. First, teachers usually want order and accountability. Second, some teachers grapple with what seems like a shifting view of the role of teacher versus the role of student. Third, as teachers, we like to be valued and needed. Let's go through each of these three, one at a time.

Order and Accountability

The last thing that a teacher wants is to set up the conditions like what we read in *The Jungle*. If you believe that self-directed learning is about chaos, disorder, and a lack of accountability; then we are not going to get very far in the conversation. In fact, as a teacher, I completely agree. We want accountability, and we do not want chaos. However, as we create more space for self-directed learning, it will challenge us to consider what it looks like to maintain order and what it means to have accountability.

This usually comes down to a matter of control. Teachers often want to know that they are still in control. They feel responsible to keep the classroom safe and a place where learning takes place. Of course, as teachers, we are often accountable for student learning as it relates to a set of standards. While some people reading this book are free from expectations about such matters, many readers are in traditional schools where failing in one or more of these areas is a recipe for disaster and maybe even for losing your job.

What is important to remember is that creating space for self-directed learning is not an either-or proposition. You can take small steps. You can begin by experimenting with a single project. Or, you can go back to the first chapter in this book where I offer a list of ideas on where to start. You can implement a personal learning network project that students work on throughout the year without changing too much else of what you do. You can begin to elicit greater student input in some of the lessons and the evaluations of what went well and what did not in the lessons. You can look for ways to invite greater student voice and choice in ways that do not detract from the standards that you are required to make the priority.

Concerns about control and accountability usually come from thinking about the more immersive examples of self-directed learning, and for those readers who have such concerns, I simply suggest that you set those more "extreme" examples aside for now. Take small steps. Just start with some ideas that allow you to maintain the control and accountability that are important to you.

With that said, after you try this for a semester or two, I encourage you to stretch yourself a little bit more, but before you try something larger, I suggest that you get online and search for schools that have more immersive self-directed learning projects. Reach out to these schools. Interview people. If they allow it and you can fit it into your schedule, try to visit the classroom or school and see it in action. Many concerns comes from struggling to envision what it would look like to have a more self-directed learning classroom, and seeing a few of them can be incredibly helpful. Of course, you want to seek out good examples, since there are certainly poorly managed examples of self-directed learning environments.

Teacher Versus Student

What is the role of the teacher and what is the role of the student? Many of us see the teacher has having the role of setting the goals, planning the lesson, directing the lesson, holding the students accountable, assessing students according to some set of standards, helping students make adequate progress in their learning, and keeping the classroom a positive and safe environment. Students have the role of coming to class prepared and ready to work, respecting the teacher and classmates, working hard, seeking the teacher's help when there is a challenge, and following instructions. At least, that is what I discovered when I conducted a random informal interview of a dozen teachers in preparation for writing this.

How does this change with more self-directed learning exercises? I argue that all of these elements still need to be present in one way or another. It is just a question of how we get there. I agree that a teacher in most schools is hired to make sure that learning happens. It is just that there are many ways for that to take place. Consider different leadership styles in a business environment. Some bosses are more hands on and others are more hands off. Most teachers see themselves as the boss of the class. While I argue that there are other equally effective ways of thinking about the role, let's just work with the boss analogy. Some bosses micromanage every aspect of the work, carefully directing each person on each task. Other bosses set a broad framework in which others work, and the boss steps in when needed. I contend that this second approach works well in the classroom also.

If you look back to the list of teacher responsibilities that I just shared, I am not suggesting that we get rid of any of those tasks. It is just a question of who takes the lead on this or what role students get to play in that regard. Assessment still needs to take place, but is it possible to involve students in the creation and/ or selection of assessments? Goals still need to be set and lessons need to be planned. To what extent can we invite students to create or co-create some of that? As such, teachers can still see themselves as ultimately in control.

I have visited enough classrooms where teachers do not think of themselves as the boss and it worked well. They took the time to help the class begin to see themselves as a democratic community with responsibilities to hold themselves and one another accountable. The might step in to guide and redirect in subtle ways, but as the community develops, and if there is a robust and working system of peer accountability, the teacher can step back and trust the community in more of these areas. Yet, that is not the case with most traditional classrooms. That might be a future aspiration, but for most classrooms, I suggest starting small.

Try a few self-directed learning efforts and see what happens. Monitor the progress. See what works; see what does not work. Do not give up after the first attempt because hardly any of us get things right the first time we try them. Could you imagine deciding to learn how to play the piano, trying to play it once, and then quitting because it did not work? Learning to play the piano takes years of practice. Learning to nurture self-directed learners takes time as well. It takes patience, persistence, practice, and a dose of humility because you will make mistakes. Yet, with persistence, this can and does work.

Being Valued

Many of us do not like to admit this, but it feels good to be wanted and valued by your students. I have spoken to plenty of teachers who directly stated that, "This is why I do what I do!" That is why so many teachers keep a box of thank you letters and words of encouragement that they receive from students over the years. Some of those treasured letters are about how students achieved goals later in life, but others are just words of appreciation. "You are the best teacher in the world!" Who does not like to be appreciated and valued by others?

Other teachers, even if we do not like to admit it, enjoy being the center of attention. Consider the fact classrooms are named after the teacher in many schools. If I had a classroom, it would be called "Dr. Bull's Classroom." The classroom is seen as my domain, and we each have ideas of what we want students to think and say about the our classroom.

"He is a hard but fair teacher, and he usually keeps things interesting."

"He is one of the kindest and most caring people that I've ever met."

"She is one of the smartest people that I know."

"If you are willing to work hard, she will make sure that you do well."

Each person might be seeking a different affirmation, but these sorts of statements become important to many of us as teachers. For that reason, moving toward self-directed learning is a change for us. We are, to some extent, sharing the stage with the students or even stepping off the stage altogether. The student becomes more central and our goal is to be only as involved as necessary. When students are learning and so engaged that they forget that the teacher is around, that is considered a success.

I at least want to acknowledge that this is a struggle for some teachers at first. At the same time, what is more rewarding for a teacher than to see a student engaged, thriving, and self-reliant? That is our focus and goal as we devote more time and attention to self-directed learning.

The Student Mindset

Another common barrier is the student mindset. Most students have grown up in a largely teacher-directed school environment. They are waiting for the teacher to tell them what to do, when to do it, and how to do it. It is common for some students to struggle as you introduce more self-directed learning opportunities. They might even make comments that cut to the heart of the teacher, statements about the teacher failing to do his or her job.

It is not wise to ignore such statements, but it is equally un- wise to just give up when this happens. Learning to be more inde- pendent and self-directed takes time and effort. It usually does not happen immediately. Remind students about this. Give students a chance to process what they are feeling and thinking. It also helps to show them examples of where they are going and what they will be able to do if they persist. You can even bring in remote guests from other classes and schools who are more self-directed in nature. Student to student mentoring can be especially helpful.

Also, it is important to note that self-directed learning is not usually about the teacher just sitting at the desk while students teach themselves. The teacher still plays an important role of coach, mentor, game or learning experience designer, facilitator of connections, and much more.

If we go back to the piano analogy that I provided earlier, you don't learn this instantly. We cannot put students in front of a piano and expect them to be able to play something perfectly the first time. If you have a classroom of students learning to play the piano, each one is going to learn at a different pace. They will each have different needs. The same thing is true with nurturing self-directed learners. Some students will embrace it right away. Others will struggle for quite a while, and you will coach and guide them along the way.

In full candor, there will be some students who may never seem to resonate with a more self-directed learning environment. Yet, these students can still learn to thrive in the classroom. The key to that is usually by building a strong and positive community. Students look out for one another. They enjoy being with and learning with one another. They mentor one another. They hold one another accountable. If you can guide students into helping create such a community, then even the students who do not seem drawn to more self-directed activities can learn and benefit from being more of such a community.

The Parent Mindset

This is not what many parents experienced in school, so some will be unaware of the benefits. Self-directed learning activities are not consistent with their experiences, and they do not know how to assess how their children are doing. Are they making progress, or are they not? One of the key ways to overcome this barrier is frequent and meaningful communication with the parents. It starts before you even try your first self-directed learning exercises in the classroom or in the school. Convey a clear vision and invite their feedback and involvement. Of course, you also want be sure to communicate the why before you start, while sharing frequent updates about what is happening, the challenges that you are facing and overcoming as a class, and the wins. Selecting pictures of students in action with a few paragraphs may be all that it takes.

It can also be helpful to provide a question an answer resource at the beginning. How will I know whether my child is making progress? What is the role of the teacher? What is the role of the student? What is the role of the parent? What is the timeline? What are they doing when and why. Then, be sure to invite parents to events where students display their work and tell stories of their learning. Invite parents to ask students questions. Of all the ways that I have seen to help students better understand the vision, these public presentations are among the most powerful.

School Policies and Practices

Depending upon the nature of the self-directed learning project or activities, you may experience challenges because of standard school policies and practices. These policies and practices were often created to support more traditional approaches to teaching and learning. Some of them will be beyond your ability to change or adjust, so you will initially need to be creative about how you can work within them. There will come a time, however, when you want to do something that does not fit the policies and practices. When this occurs, it is time to work with school leadership. Share your vision, the compelling reason, and what you think is needed to be successful. If you engage leadership in your smaller and earlier exercises, inviting input and involvement, then these larger conversations are much easier. Sometimes this will just emerge naturally over time.

Of course, some school leaders might not be as supportive at first. While respecting the policies, you can persist in trying to make a compelling case for why you think this is important for your students. You can take time to listen and learn from concerns and critiques. You can respect the wishes of leadership while finding small but significant ways to engage students in owning their learning and playing and active role in co-creating the learning experiences.

There are limitations to what you can do in a traditional school context with self-directed learning, but your smaller efforts are not insignificant. When you go to a fully self-directed school where students can immerse themselves in a single project for weeks and months, it is inspiring and amazing to see the maturity and engagement of the learners. You might not see the same depth and level of transformation, but you can still help students make good progress. Even if you never experience that more immersive models, your slow and steady efforts to nurture self-direction in your classroom is an important part of preparing your students for the future. Simply making small changes that invite students into setting goals, planning lessons, and devising feedback plans can go a long way in nurturing the mindset of a lifelong self-directed learner. You can even do this within the most traditional policies and school practices.

Intrinsic Motivation[2]

A common challenge is the concern about student motivation. What about the students who just sit round and do nothing? Of course, this is just as possible with self-directed learning as it is with many other forms of teaching and learning. However, it is a legitimate concern even thought, in my experience, it is far less common than some fear. As such, I like to approach to concern by referring to the broader concept of motivation.

As we already explored in this chapter, not every student in a project-based or self-directed learning environment will be excited about this new model. It takes more effort. It is counter to many of the school success strategies learned through years of a traditional model. There are often new skills, disciplines and dispositions that one needs to nurture to get the most of out of these experiences. Nonetheless, almost everyone has been engaged by a project-based or self-directed learning experience at some point in life. As a result, teachers in self-directed environments quickly learn that calling an activity self-directed or giving students greater

2. Much of this section originally comes from an article that I published called, "Surfacing Intrinsic Motivation in Project-Based and Self-Directed Learning Environments."

choice does not magically change the classroom culture. Not every student instantly gets excited about the idea of getting immersed or even lost in a project or inquiry.

To address this, I find it helpful to go back to instructional design basics. In fact, I still return to Lepper and Malone's 1987 chapter on "Making Learning Fun: A Taxonomy of Intrinsic Motivations for Learning."[3] In this chapter, they outline six types of intrinsic motivators for learning: challenge, curiosity, power, fantasy, cooperation and competition, and recognition. They offer teachers (and students) ways to think about addressing low motivation while still advocating for the growth and development of self-directed learners.

1. Challenge

A student tends to be more intrinsically motivated when there is a right challenge fit. Csikszentmihalyi writes about this in his work on *Flow*.[4] Challenge is not simply about deciding what is the right level of challenge for a student. There is more subjectivity it. A student may have immense competence in an area but lose motivation when having to work on a challenge that is well within her abilities. That is because challenge is more about the learner's perception of both the challenge and her own skills related to that challenge.

Understanding a student's self-esteem becomes important in finding the right challenge fit. We begin to address challenge by helping learners establish goals that are appropriately challenging, but have a stretch element to them. A measure of uncertainty about whether one can accomplish the goal can help with motivation, granted that it is not too much uncertainty. We want a goal that is the right level of challenge, difficult enough to be worthy of pursuit, but not so difficult as to instill a sense of certain failure.

Also, when working with students who are new to self-directed learning, it is useful to start with shorter term goals. Just like it can be helpful for an aspiring marathoner to start with the

---

3. Lepper and Malone, "Making Learning Fun," 223–53.

4. Csikszentmihalyi, *Flow and the Foundations of Positive Psychology*.

goal of a 5K, it is helpful for a student to begin with a shorter term project. Without hope of success, motivation plummets, so figuring out challenge becomes critical. Feedback also becomes important. If students are uncertain about their ability to face a challenge, more frequent feedback may be necessary at first to help build confidence. Keep in mind, however, that low self-esteem in academic areas may have built up for over a decade, so a few days or weeks will probably not be enough to help build the confidence to embrace and overcome significant academic challenges. Given this fact, small but significant self-directed learning wins will help students build the confidence to face larger challenges.

There is another element to this in some environments, and that is the confidence drop that comes from seeing other students work on projects that seem more significant. In a traditional class, some students get higher grades than others, but everyone is generally working on the same things. In a self-directed learning environment, the wide spectrum of student projects becomes clear. This can motivate and inspire some students while demotivating others. There is still benefit in these comparisons (as I will mention later), but beware of the impact on self-esteem as well.

2. Curiosity

Lepper and Malone distinguish between two types of curiosity: sensory and cognitive.[5] The first has to do with the physical senses. As such, it is useful to ask if the learning spaces and the available learning resources are stimulating. How are the senses engaged? This is why Maria Montessori's philosophy of education pays so much attention to the environment and the learning resources in that environment. Take a few minutes and browse the web for images of Montessori classrooms. It does not take long to get the idea. Cognitive curiosity, however, relates to the drive for us to make sense of things. When we are convinced that we do not have a clear understanding of something that is important to us or that our

5. Lepper and Malone, 235.

understanding is incomplete, that can conjure cognitive curiosity. Or, if something in our thinking is inconsistent with reality, that too evokes curiosity.[6]

Learning to ask questions that spark curiosity is, therefore, a valuable skill for teacher and student. This is not just an exercise in creating lists of interesting questions about a subject. If it is going to awaken intrinsic motivation through curiosity, it must be about surfacing inconsistencies, incompleteness, and a lack of clarity about something of personal importance to the learner.

3. Control

As with challenge, we are not just talking about the objective measure of control given to students in the learning environment. We are referring to the perceived amount of control. The perception of control impacts motivation more than the reality of it.[7] If you see unmotivated learners in a context, what is their perception of control?

One way to get at this is to make sure student choice is available, choice about what questions to pursue and how to pursue them. This does not mean making everything completely open-ended, as that can overwhelm (think back to challenge) and de-motivate. Lepper and Malone suggest that 5–7 choices is ideal for many environments. Or, if there are unlimited choices, it will help to offer clear guidance on how to narrow things down.[8] Regardless, giving choice or increasing the perception of choice elevates intrinsic motivation.

Related to choice is also the concept of power, where a learner's choices have obvious and significant implications. When a learner can see that her choices made a large difference, this impacts motivation. This is another reason feedback and shorter projects can help build intrinsic motivation, because both are ways to show the impact of a person's individual choices.[9]

6. Ibid, 236.
7. Ibid, 238.
8. Ibid, 239.
9. Ibid, 239.

4. Fantasy

In the original chapter by Lepper and Malone, their reference to fantasy is in the context of games and learning, so my reflection here may deviate well beyond their intended use of the term.[10] Malone worked from the following definition of fantasy, "mental images of things not present to the senses or within the actual experience of the person involved."[11] This can be effective with teacher-directed project-based learning by building a project into an immersive fantasy experience. It can also be used for more self-directed projects. Many teachers find great success creating launch events for new projects that incorporate fantasy and imagination as a framework for the projects.

Helping students learn how to use their imagination with regard to projects can also be a powerful motivator. Invite students to imagine the potential impact of their project upon one or more people. Encourage students to use fantasy and imagination as they work on their projects. They might, for example, create fictional characters for whom they are designing the project.

5. Cooperation and Competition

While I rarely think about leveraging competition in my classroom, there are ways that people do so in self-directed learning contexts, like having students pitch ideas, and a panel rates their performance, perhaps giving a first, second and third place. Or, there might be a more objective element of competition, with people or groups competing to create an object that has the largest impact in some way. Think of projects where groups are given $10 with the goal of having the greatest social impact with the money. Or, there are the popular projects around protecting an egg with some sort of design, or creating a paper airplane that can fly the greatest distance.

10. Malone's work in the 1980s on fantasy is also a worthwhile read. While he developed his ideas over time, a useful starting point is his original doctoral dissertation on the subject, *What Makes Things Fun to Learn?*

11. Malone and Lepper, 56.

Similarly, charging entire classes or groups to work together in the accomplishment of a significant challenge or socially relevant project can be a powerful motivator. This sense of team can be incredibly motivating for students, especially at certain developmental stages.

In fact, even in instances where the project and learning itself seems to be a bit less motivating for some students, building a positive, fun, and encouraging community of learners can make up the difference. Many students are highly social by nature, and they just consider doing the work a responsibility of membership in that community. While the ideal is for every student to love the learning itself, it is unwise to ignore this deeply social reality. If you can help nurture a positive community where students support one another, value their learning, and pass that on to one another; then you are well on your way to building a world-class self-directed learning community.

6. Recognition

This may seem like extrinsic motivation, but Lepper and Malone describe recognition as intrinsic because it comes from a need for approval or recognition. This is an area that is often highlighted by project-based learning advocates, noting the benefit of an authentic audience for the product. However, recognition can also be used throughout the process by making learner progress, discoveries and developments more visible to the community throughout the learning experience. A class blog, practice presentations, frequent show and tell exercises, a scheduled public exhibition, and the like build opportunities for recognition throughout the self-directed learning process. Adding these into the design is consistently ranked as a high-impact strategy among those who are striving to build more self-directed learning communities.

Motivation Conclusion

Self-directed learning environments have many exciting possibilities and affordances, but they do not usually happen by chance. Teachers still play a valuable role in designing spaces and contexts that lead to motivation. Teachers can construct motivating learning challenges and experiences, and helping students learn to motivate themselves. As such, the six items mentioned in the prior pages provide you with a good starting place.

Barrier Conclusions

This is no short and easy list of challenges and barriers. Promoting self-directed learning is hard and persistent work because our education system as a whole does not place a priority on it. Many of the policies, practices, norms, and elements that we value enough to measure are not connected to self-directed learning. Yet, with time and effort, you can be a champion for self-directed learning in ways that truly benefit your students. These are certainly easy barriers to overcome, especially given that most of them are mindset barriers, but progress is both rewarding and achievable. It begins with working through the barriers challenges that exist in our own minds, then working with other key stakeholders to help them discover the power and possibility of nurturing competence and confidence as a self-directed learner. Keep the goal front and center, as well as a compelling reason. Then start planning and building a community that helps to work through these and related challenges one by one.

7

The Self-Directed Learning Friendly Classroom and School

LET'S GET TO THE nuts and bolts, the classroom. Self-directed learning can happen in homeschool environments. It can happen outside of school. It can happen in school. If a student is in a traditional school, and we want to embrace self-directed learning, it has to impact what happens in the daily classroom. So, how do we create a self-directed friendly classroom? It starts with something that I talked about in the last chapter. A self-directed friendly classroom is one where the teacher understands the role and the value of self-directed learning. It is one where the teacher has worked through some of the concerns and the fears, the barriers. It is also one where the teacher helps create specific opportunities for students to engage in more self-directed learning, which will be the focus of this chapter. Following are specific steps that you can take to create a classroom where students are progressing toward greater competence and confidence as self-directed learners.

[Inviting Students Behind the Scenes]

Using the metaphor of a theater, where do you picture students in the learning process? Are they the actors on the stage? Or, are they the people in the audience, enjoying the performance of the teacher? Or, maybe the students are the playwrights, the directors, the actors, the critic sitting it the audience, or maybe members of the tech crew. The more traditional answer might be that students are either the audience members or the actors following the instructions of the director. When we begin to think about how to nurture self-directed learning, we are envisioning a classroom where students experience many or all of these roles at one time or another. Students are invited into the audience, but they are also invited behind the scene. They are even invited to help write the plays in which they act.

As such, a great starting point in the classroom is taking the lesson plan and putting it in front of the students. It is inviting students to be partners in the design of the lesson. You are recognizing that the classroom is not your classroom as the teacher, but the class belongs to the community. The community has say about what is learned and how it is learned. Individuals are also given a growing measure of input on those questions that we have visited repeatedly in this text. What do I need to learn? How will I learn it? How will I monitor my progress? How will I know when I have learned it?

They say that the best way to learn something is to teach it, so what we are talking about here is sharing, at least in some ways, the role of teacher with the students. You are inviting them to see themselves as co-learners with you as well as co-teachers and co-creators of the learning experiences. As you do this, you will discover that the spirit of self-directed learner will begin to grow in your classroom. You will be well on your way to becoming a self-directed friendly classroom. In the following section, we will look at each of these questions in a bit more detail, considering how you can involve students even if you cannot or do not want to hand over full control to the students.

What do I need to learn?

You are probably in a context where you have predefined answers to this question in the form of learning objectives and academic standards. Alongside that, you can also invite the students to establish some of their own personal or group goals. This gives students a chance to put their individual and collective imprint on the lesson. Greater voice will eventually lead to greater ownership.

How will I learn it?

Even if there is little to not flexibility on the learning objectives, the standards, and the learning goals; most teachers have greater discretion on how students meet the standards. As the teacher, you probably have ideas on how to teach a given concept, but why not involve students into deciding this? Perhaps they can help you come up with more effective and engaging ways to approach a common topic. They might help you design projects, games, problem-based learning experiences, and they might help curate online and other resources related to the subject.

What would be the absolute best way for us to meet this learning goal? Invite the students into dreaming up creative and interesting answers to this question. Why not make it imaginative and fun? Imagine that you are preparing the next generation of neurosurgeons, and you want to equip them to conduct brain surgery in a way that removes a tumor and the patient survives. What is the absolute best way to learn how to do that? What is the most effective way to teach or learn this? Well, I would suggest that it is probably to find people with brain tumors, bring them into the classroom, and let students conduct surgeries on the people over and over until they get it right.

Obviously, we have an ethical problem with that approach. So, that is not realistic, so then we muse about the next best option. Maybe it is observing others conducting surgery with a person who is pointing out exactly what is happening and how it is happening, and then you get to try it out in a simulated environment. Maybe it is not on a real patient, but it is on some sort of machine or simulated brain on a computer. Well, maybe these are not realistic, either, because you do not have the resources. No matter. Your goal is to invite the students into this conversation about the most authentic and effective way to learn something. Let the students join you in the creation of the learning experiences because, if you have a class of twenty, that is an impressive collection of minds. You will come up with great ideas, the students will experience the job of co-creating, and student engagement is likely to increase.

Know that at first, at least in most classrooms, you are not going to give the students all of the say, but you are giving them a little more voice and choice than they had before. Over time, you can gradually increase the amount of voice and choice that you give students, empowering them with growing levels of confidence and competence as self-directed learners. Put them into research teams, and send them out in advance of a unit to figure out creative resources and ways that they could learn something. Have them bring ideas back that they can propose to the class.

I recall one example of a teacher who decided that she was not going to use a social studies textbook. Instead, she and the students opted to co-create a social studies textbook, and the students collectively started to figure out all of these facts and issues about history as they wrote a text. They did it in the form of a wiki. That is a great example of how to embrace self-directed learning while still meeting the same basic learning objectives and academic standards. The students found themselves going out and interviewing experts. They interviewed professors, scientists, government leaders, and other key figures as an integrated part of their study. They found great resources. They learned to analyze these resources, to fact-check them, and they started discovering ideas unlikely to emerge from a single teacher.

How will I monitor my progress and how will I know when I have learned it?

Just as with the questions about learning goals and the lesson plan, we can also engage students in planning and designing feedback and assessments. Students can learn to create a blend of feedback from the teacher, from external experts, from their peers, from computer software, and even from themselves. By inviting students into the design and selection of feedback and assessment mechanisms, students will also eventually begin to see that the role of feedback is to help them progress in their learning, not just to give them a grade. Too often, students go through class thinking of quizzes, tests, and assignments as little more than a means of assigning them a grade. Somewhere along the way, they lose sight of the fact that all of this is supposed to be in the service of learning and growth. The more that we can engage students in the design, the more they will be able to see and internalize the proper purpose and role of feedback and assessment. This is not about being rated and ranked. It is about growing and pursuing your best.

"How I Did It" Show and Tell

We often think of show and tell as that childhood school activity where students bring an object to school. One at a time, students take turns sharing about the object and what it means to the them. Students get to know one another. They are practicing public speaking in a simple and informal way. It is also a chance for the teacher to get to know the students in a new way. Yet, we can also use a very similar activity with any age or group of learners as a way to celebrate small examples of self-directed learning.

We can surface and celebrate self-directed learning when students are in a class with traditional tests, working on individual or group projects, or they are working on any type of homework or learning experience. The goal is to get students talk to one another about how they are self-blending, what strategies and tools they are using while working in class. For example, one student might have performed very well on a test. Maybe it became public knowledge. Too often, such success is attributed to just being a smart student. It reinforces the idea that some students are born with a special ability while others are not. While acknowledging the role of genetics, there are so many other factors that contribute to student success. We know that learning how to study effectively can improve student test scores. We know that learning to conduct research and write a research paper is something that students can learn and improve over time. The problem is that we too often focus on what is learned and accomplished, but not how it is learned and accomplished.

This is where show and tell comes to the rescue. When a teacher sees a student improving significantly from one assignment to the next, why not talk to that student about possibly sharing her story with the class. What did she do differently this time and how did it help? When a student completes an impressive project or paper, ask this student to share how he goes about researching and writing. What methods and strategies does he use and why? How does he conduct the research? How does he stay organized? What challenges did he face and how did he overcome them?

There is so much for students to learn from one another, and creating show and tell moments like this can quickly begin to demystify learning. Students begin to see that learning is a set of skills that we can develop other time. They become reflective about how they learn. They discover how much their habits and choices can impact their learning and their performance in school.

Some students might not be ready to volunteer right away, but you can start by simply looking for examples, pulling those students aside, and privately asking if they would consider sharing with the class. Some will decline, but once a few students accept the invitation, you can begin to build important momentum. In fact, those who are sharing come to see how their sharing benefits classmates while also being recognized for a job well done. At the same time, the rest of the class gets to learn from that student. Over time, these show and tell experiences can be rich and engaging question-and-answer exchanges, helping to build a stronger culture of self-directed learning even in otherwise largely teacher-directed classrooms.

The Personal Learning Network

We already dedicated an entire chapter to this topic, but I include it once more as a reminder, because it one of the easier but more impactful ways to help students move toward greater ownership and awareness. Without changing anything else in a class, you can invite students to create a log of the people, resources, and technologies that they are using to learn. Provide time for students to share about their network with others. Offer them guidance on how to refine and expand their network to achieve different goals.

Doing this over a full school year or even multiple years is a good way give students one more way to think about their personal role and responsibility for learning. Of course, this should be something meaningful for students. If students just see it as busy work or disconnected from everything else, then they are unlikely to learn anything from such an activity.

The Self-Directed Learning Project

If you can find the time, there is also the opportunity to provide opportunity for students to create their own learning agenda. I found great success with a simple template that I have used with college students, and others are using it with students in elementary school, middle school, and high school. The template simply includes a series of questions.

What is my driving question?
What is the question that will drive my inquiry?

Invite students to pick something that is personally compelling, something that matters to them. This can be a single question, but it is one of the more important parts of the project. If it is not a question with which a student resonates, then it will be much harder for the student to get immersed in the project. Many teachers find that it is useful to facilitate activities and exercises where students study great questions and inquires from the past, perhaps from students in other schools. The teacher guides a conversation about what sorts of questions are more powerful and provocative than others. As such, this is not just about writing down a question and moving on. Students can benefit from grappling with and workshopping their questions with classmates over days or maybe even a couple of weeks in some cases. Getting the right question will go a long way for making the project a success.

How will I pursue answers to this question?

This might include readings, ideas for field trips, experiments, interviews, new experiences, research, a review of research, building a personal learning network related to their question, or perhaps joining one or more online communities. Students get to decide upon the learning journey in many ways, but as with framing the question, this is something that benefits from small and large group exploration and discussion. Students can learn from curated resources and one another as they consider the best and most useful ways to go about exploring their questions. Remember that this is going to be new for many students at first, so it will take them time to learn how to do this well.

How will I document & reflect on my learning journey?

I often suggest that this should be in a form that the teacher can review at any point in the journey. It gives the teacher a chance to monitor the student's learning. I usually ask students to update it at least twice a week. Sometimes the platform is selected by the teacher, like in a designated Google document that the student shares with the teacher. In other cases, students may have the choice on where and how they do this. It might be a shared online document, a blog, a video diary, or maybe so other creative but reflective expressing of their learning and progress.

What culminating product(s)/project(s)/performance(s) will be the result of my work?

Possibilities include but are not limited to papers, presentations to different audiences, models, photo journals, events that you plan and host, things that students design or create, or anything else that provides evidence of learning. In addition to answering this question, students have the challenge of communicating what they learned as a result of this project, project, or performance.

How will I monitor my progress and get feedback on my progress throughout the project?

One possibility is to have peers, teachers, or experts frequently review and give feedback based on what students are sharing. Students may also want to schedule "checkup" meetings with people who can help give feedback, including the teacher. Instead of the teacher setting all of this up for the students, it is powerful when students learn to plan their own feedback systems, albeit with help from peers and the teacher as a coach.

What is the tentative timeline for this project?

There are usually certain parameters set by the school or teacher. It might be a four to six week project. It could also be a semester or longer. Many students benefit from working within some set of parameters or structure, but this is also a great chance for students to learn time management by planning and setting at least some of the benchmarks along the way. Yet, even in some of the more self-directed schools, I often see teacher-dedicated checkpoints as often as two or three times a week, or as infrequent as once every week or two. Especially as students are just beginning to direct their own learning, a few parameters keep the student from falling into that dangerous trap of procrastinating on everything until the last week or two.

What are some key resources to get started?

While an earlier question asked students to begin to identify some of the resources and activities that will be used during the project, I found it helpful to also invite them to start with a few starting points. As they work through these, they will likely come up with new ideas that help them move forward and refine their work. These starting resources might include a key person to interview, a core text, or a few select articles. While students are doing much of this work on their own, the teacher and others can offer tips and guidance on where to go and how to decide upon these initial resources.

How will this project connect with one or more key standards or learning outcomes?

This last question is usually important in more traditional school contexts. There are usually certain standards that need to be met or focused upon in a class. As such, this last question give students a chance to align with they want to learn with what they need to learn based upon the standard. Yet, this is also a place where the teacher might find a need to contribute something.

What is the role of the teacher?

At this point in the text, it should be apparent that a move toward self-directed learning is not necessarily a decrease in work for the teacher. Rather, it is a change in the nature of work. The teacher becomes a coach, mentor, and learning experience designer. The teacher is constantly observing, being deeply curious about the students, what is working, and what is not working. The teacher is helping to facilitate thought and student-to-student interaction that empowers student voice and deepens their learning journey.

The goal is for students to become increasingly independent, but self-directed learning is not about solitary learning. Similarly, while self-directed learning is about learners becoming increasingly independent, it does not necessarily suggest independent learning. It can be highly interdependent, collaborative, and cooperative. Furthermore, the reality is that learners in a given context will likely have varying levels of competence and confidence with self-direction, especially those who spent years in a learning context that was dominated by a teacher-directed approach to learning.

Even for students with significant confidence, a self-directed learning approach does not devalue the role of experts, mentors, coaches and guides. Self-directed learning is more about how people learn, and about how to create an environment where that learning can flourish. It elevates the role of the learner, recognizes that learning happens when the individual learner takes ownership for her own learning.

A teacher/mentor can play a valuable role as one engages in self-directed learning. Roger Hiemstra, a scholar of adult learning and self-directed learning, addressed this question in "Self-Directed Learning: Individualizing Instruction– Most Still Do It Wrong!" In his essay, he proposes six roles of the teacher: content resource, resource locator, interest stimulator, positive attitude generator, creativity and critical thinking stimulator, and evaluation stimulator.[1] In other words, the teacher helps to cultivate an environment that is conducive to self-directed learning, and provides assistance for individuals and groups of learners. As drawn from Hiemstra's six roles, following is a short reflection on each of them. These provide a sense of the types of thoughts and actions that occupy a teacher's time in an increasingly self-directed environment. As you can see, this is far from a hands-off role.

Content Resource and Content Locator

The teacher helps to make accessible and available rich content and resources that will benefit individual learners. This content might be digital, traditional texts, artifacts, experiential, help coordinating visits and interviews, or it might simply be conversational (content acquired through dialogue with the teacher, peers or others). This role of teacher as content resource and resource locator is also sometimes referred to as a curator of content. Of course, as students become increasingly competent and confident, they will also take on this role in growing measure.

Interest Stimulator and Positive Attitude Generator

The teacher aids the learner as she grows in confidence and competence with information and research literacy. Googling an idea may be helpful, but there are many other valuable ways to explore a topic. The teacher can help learners develop these skills in many ways, including coordinating opportunities for learners to share and guide one another (peer-to-peer learning).

1. Hiemstra, "Self-directed Learning," 46–59.

Critical Thinking Stimulator

The teacher provides guidance and outlets for critical thinking, brainstorming, and various types of creative thinking. Hiemstra talks about this in terms of helping learners engage in outlets that help with critical and creative thinking (different forms of journaling, reflective writing for an audience as may occur with blogging or contributing to a wiki, engaging in small group discussions, workshopping, etc.). I also see opportunity for the teacher to offer opportunities for learners to explore specific mind tools (things like the SCAMPER approach to creative thinking).[2]

Evaluation Stimulator

The teacher helps the learner to engage in an evaluative process, assisting the learner as he identifies ways to check his progress toward certain goals, and establishes ways to evaluate the benefits and limitations of his work. This can start with feedback as each learner produces a learning contract. Yet again, over time, there is greater opportunity for students to play increasing roles in this evaluative process. Note that the role of evaluation stimulator is not evaluator. It is about prompting evaluation, helping the learners to take on this role for themselves as much as is possible in your learning context.

---

2. SCAMPER is a common mnemonic that stands for substitute, combine, modify, adapt, put to another use, eliminate, and reserve. It is a creative thinking tool that helps you to look at problems or issues from unique perspectives. For example, if you are thinking about reducing pollution, you might draw from the SCAMPER words to ask questions like: What if we combined the idea of reducing pollution with the mechanics of a video game? What if we tried to elimate pollution by creating more products that self-destruct? Or, what if adapted laws to reward people who reduced pollution instead of enforcing laws for people who contributed to it? Of course, not every question is helpful or will lead to a superior solution, but I find this tool to be useful in looking at ideas and issues from fresh perspectives.

Other Roles

Hiemstra also describes the teacher as having a helpful role with regard to the social, emotional, and psychological aspects of the learner experience; offering experiences that might aid with motivation and confidence-building, for example.[3]

Note that all of this can be done without turning the environment back into a teacher-directed experience. The teacher is not doing these things to or for a learner, but providing guidance and help as the learner does them. Consider, for example, the role of a librarian. It is not usually the role of the librarian to decide the research topic, conduct the research, or even to formally evaluate the work of the patron. However, a great reference librarian is a tremendous guide and resource. I am not suggesting that the role of teacher and librarian are the same in a self-directed learning environment, but there are at least a few similarities. The teacher who is devoted to these tasks will have more than enough good and important work to do. The main focus is simply upon being a guide as students grow in their capacity for self-directed learning.

Of course, as we consider throughout this text, we can think of self-directed learning on a spectrum. In some environments, the teacher might also play some of the more traditional roles. In other contexts, the teacher is striving to hand off as much responsibility as possible to the students. In either of these situations, however, the types of roles described in this section will usually need to be fulfilled by someone if we want to see success. This is especially true when we are first building a culture of self-directed learning in the classroom.

The Self-blending Friendly School is the Distributed School

So far in this chapter, we explored becoming a self-blended-friendly classroom. What about the even larger picture? How do you become a self-blended-friendly school? In some ways, the classroom

3. Ibid, 57.

is much easier because all it really takes is one teacher committed to working with a willing group of students in that classroom. You can can start to embrace personal learning networks. You can start to do personalized learning projects that are an extensions and different ways of thinking about research projects that have been used for years and years in classrooms. You can do them in small and significant ways for the students. Yet, what if you want to become a more self-directed learning school? What does that take?

Getting Informed and Clarifying Mission

The first steps involve getting informed about the possibilities and developing a shared mission. This idea is hard for some to imagine until they see it in action. Watching some good video examples are a starting point, but nothing replaces finding a way to visit classrooms and schools that are more self-directed. Interview teachers, founders, students, parents, and others can be incredibly enlightening, and I find this to be one of the fastest ways to work through common concerns and misconceptions. Yet, as the possibilities become more evident to the community, then it is time to come together and decide how these examples can and will inform what happens in the school.

If you do not have the leaders and the teachers on board with this, a shared vision or mission for where you are going, you can wander aimlessly. The same thing is true in the world of educational technology. Educational technology without a compelling mission and vision, without a compelling reason, is just chasing shiny objects.

I remember hearing a story about how you can catch a raccoon. It sounds like a cruel kind of trap, and I am not sure if it actually works. I have been told it does. You take an old log and drill a hole in it, just smaller than the size of a raccoon's fist. Then you can take a couple of nails and put them in at an angle on the sides of the hole. Finally, you take a shiny coin or object, and you put it in hole. Supposedly, the raccoon will see that shiny object, reach down, grab the coin, and try to pull it out. Yet, the fist clenched around the object along with the nails makes it a trap for the raccoon. All the raccoon has to do to escape is just let go of the coin. Yet, the raccoon refuses to do this. It will just hold on to this shiny object. Which goal is more important: your life or holding on to a shiny coin?

The same thing can actually happen in schools as well, if you are just chasing the next shiny trend or innovation, including self-blended and self-directed learning, it can be a trap, preventing you from achieving your mission. If you do not have a compelling mission, you do not know how to prioritize opportunities. You can get trapped, running into more than a few problems along the way.

This is why we need to have deep, substantive conversations with all the key stakeholders. Explore together the definition of self-directed learning, why we are doing this, why it matters for our students, and make your own list of questions. Do not give up until you have all relentlessly explored and found meaningful answers to those questions, until you have a shared vision for what you want to do and why you want to do it.

You do not need to have everything perfectly figured out, but if you can have that clear mission and a clear set of values that are going drive what you do and why you do it, then you are setting your community up for success.

Experimentation

The next step is to start building a culture of experimentation. You don't just become a self-directed learning school. This is culture that you build over time, and it calls for humility and experimentation. You will not get everything right the first time. There will be confusion and challenges. People want to be prepared for this reality, having a culture that tolerates, even embraces such a reality.

There are certainly models where you can take what worked in one school and try to plop it into another school, but usually, the culture is different, and it does not work as you expected. You can use some of the same basic operating principles, but other parts need to be co-created within your school. This allows you to co-create something that is designed upon the uniqueness of your school.

The Student Role

Start with the role of the learners. If self-directed learning is about equipping students for having greater agency, voice, and choice; about preparing them to be independent and interdependent citizens; then we are wise to start thinking about the role of students in the community. How can they play a role in co-creating this new culture? How can they be involved in planning, key decisions, monitoring the progress, and so much more? This is intimidating for some school leaders who are used to directing students more than involving them, but making this shift early in the process is one of the fastest ways to make progress. It might be awkward and somewhat messy at times, but if we can agree to affirm the insights and leadership of students in shaping their own learning community, then we know that we are going in the right direction.

Monitoring Progress

In my study of high-impact learning organizations, I consistently find that the most innovative and impactful organizations are addicted to monitoring how they are doing. This is something that people are constantly doing. They do it daily, weekly, monthly, quarterly, and annually. They seek insights from parents, students, teachers, and any other stakeholder who might give them useful input. Sometimes it is more informal data collection through observing and asking questions. In other cases it is more formal or more quantitative. The key is to genuinely seek candid insights about what is working and what is not. Then we work with the community to respond to the data that we collect. Of course, this is not just for self-directed learning environments. This works for all types of school cultures.

Analysis of Policies, Processes, and Practices

If we are talking about an existing school, most of the school is not built around self-directed learning. As such, there are policies, processes, and preferred practices that probably do not support our newly defined mission and values related to self-directed learning. If we do not take steps to work on collectively adjusting these, then we will find ourselves constantly running into the brick walls of resistant policies and practices. Of course, this might involve support from board members, teachers, students, and parents; but it is necessary if we are going to move forward. It might mean revisiting our grading system, our daily schedule, our course requirements, how we measure progress and success, what we reward and celebrate in the school, the curricula, our conduct policies, the silos of distinct classes and subjects, and any number of topics. We do not necessarily need to change all or any of these overnight, but we must be aware of how each of this support or detract from our goal of being a self-directed learning friendly school. Then we need to come together to discuss how we will respond. If we do not engage in this important work, any school-wide effort in self-directed learning is likely to diminish over time. We are trying to pour new wine in old wineskins, and all that does is create an impending mess.

Concluding Thoughts
about Becoming Self-Directed Learning Friendly

There are countless ways to move forward. The inspired teacher can get started today. You can take small, daily steps toward investing in student agency. Of course, this chapter also gives you a starting point for making larger scale changes in an individual classroom or the larger school. There is no one perfect way to go about it. In my study and experience, what matters is having a clear sense of what you want to accomplish and why, to commit to this for the long-term given the time and experimentation involved, and it invest in building a culture that is conducive to it. You will learn the rest along the way. It is a challenging adventure, but I suspect that, if you persist, you will also join countless others in saying that it is well worth it.

8

Conclusion

THANK YOU FOR JOINING me on the learning journey of going through this book and exploring self-directed learning. I am genuinely humbled and grateful that you opted to share a few hours of your life with me to consider these ideas. We started with foundational questions about the definition of self-directed learning. We explored the why of self-directed learning. We examined how this affects access and opportunity. We also reflected on why this connected age calls for such a change in our classrooms and schools. Then we looked at how to overcome common obstacles, and how we can take specific steps to nurture self-directed learning in our classrooms and schools. I suppose the only thing left is for you to decide if and how you want to join this movement, how you want to start nurturing student agency in your classroom, school, in your family, and in your own life and learning.

As I promised at the beginning of the text, I did not give you a step-by-step guide because I am not convinced that such a guide works, nor do I see it as resonating with the spirit of self-directed learning. You can learn from exemplars and research. You can benchmark from others. You can gather insights and input from countless sources. In the end, it is important to make it your own and to invite those in your learning community to join in co-creating something that matters to that community.

Too often in education, experts arise on every possible topic. They establish themselves as the guardians of right and wrong practice. There is indeed research to guide our practice that we are wise to consider. At the same time, this is an art as much as it is a science. We are not building a factory. We are nurturing a community. Experts will want to tell you that you are not doing true self-directed learning, that your light version is a distortion or an abomination. Still others will tell you that you are too extreme. These comments are not as much about what you are doing as they are about these other individual's personal beliefs and values. My advice is to listen and learn from these different viewpoints (including the ones shared in this book), but to not necessarily follow their advice as if it were some mandate from on high. You can take it under advisement, but it is your learning community's task to experiment and learn together. You are co-creators of the learning community, and I contend that this process of co-creating is more important than exactly how it fits with current models elsewhere. You are accountable to one another and the external key stakeholders (board, community, external agencies, your core convictions, and your moral responsibility in education), and these will certainly inform what you do and how you do it.

You, the learners and other key stakeholders are at an important moment in history. This connected age in which we find ourselves in changing how we live, think, work, play, connect, and learn. The amazing part is that we are just at the beginning of these changes. While we can make informed speculation about what will come next, nobody is certain. What I do know is that the future is not just something that happens to us. We are agents of change, which is why I believe so strongly in nurturing human agency. I see it as fundamental to creating a more humane learning ecosystem and society. As Denis Gabor wrote, "Futures cannot be predicted, but futures can be created."[1] If this is true, then I believe that a fundamental need for education in a free society is to equip and empower learners who embrace the challenge and opportunity to

1. Gabor, *Inventing Education for the Future*, 207.

be co-creators of our future, and I believe that a growing emphasis upon self-directed learning in our schools can help us achieve that. If you agree, then I welcome you to this wonderful adventure into self-directed learning.

Bibliography

Bull, Bernard. "The Boy Who Wanted to be a Mortician When he Grew Up." Etale, December 21, 2016, http://etale.org/main/2016/12/21/12731/.

———. "Surfacing Intrinsic Motivation in Project-Based and Self-Directed Learning Environments." Etale. November 1, 2014, http://etale.org/main/2014/11/01/surfacing-intrinsic-motivation-in-project-based-self-directed-learning-envioronments/.

———. *What Really Matters? Ten Critical Issues in Contemporary Education.* Eugene: Wipf & Stock, 2016.

Church, Kathryn. *Forbidden Narratives: Critical Autobiography As Social Science.* Australia: Gordon and Breach, 1995.

Cross, Jay. *Informal Learning: Rediscovering the Natural Pathways That Inspire Innovation and Performance.* San Francisco, CA: Jossey-Bass, 2007.

Csikszentmihalyi, Mihaly. *Flow and the Foundations of Positive Psychology: The Collected Works of Mihaly Csikszentmihalyi.* Dordrecht: Springer, 2014.

Freire, Paulo. *Pedagogy of the Oppressed.* New York: Continuum, 2000.

French, Michael T, Jenny F Homer, Ioana Popovici, and Philip K Robins.. "What You Do in High School Matters: High School GPA, Educational Attainment, and Labor Market Earnings As a Young Adult." *Eastern Economic Journal* 41, no. 3 (2015) 370–86.

Gabor, Dennis. *Inventing Education for the Future.* Los Angeles: Institute of Government and Public Affairs, University of California, 1965.

Gardner, Howard. *Frames of Mind: The Theory of Multiple Intelligences.* New York, NY: Basic, 1993.

Gibbons, M. *The Self-Directed Learning Handbook: Challenging Adolescent Students to Excel.* San Francisco: Jossey-Bass, 2002.

Hawking, Stephen, and Nelson Runger. *A Brief History of Time.* Prince Frederick, MD: Recorded, 2014.

Hiemstra, R. "Self-Directed Learning." In *The Sourcebook for Self-Directed Learning*, edited by Rothwell, William J., and Kevin J. Sensenig, 9–20. Amherst, Massachusetts: HRD Pess, 1999.

Hiemstra, R. "Self-directed Learning: Individualizing Instruction—Most Still Do it Wrong!" *International Journal of Self-Directed Learning* 8.1 (2011) 46–59.

Holt, John. *How Children Learn*. Boston: Da Capo Press Inc, 2011.

Kleon, Austin. *Show Your Work! 10 Ways to Share Your Creativity and Get Discovered*. New York: Workman, 2014.

Knowles, Malcolm S. *Self-Directed Learning: A Guide for Learners and Teachers*. Englewood Cliffs, NJ: Prentice Hall Regents, 1980.

Malone, Thomas, and Mark Lepper. "Making Learning Fun: A Taxonomy of Intrinsic Motivation for Learners." In *Aptitude, Learning, and Instruction*, edited by Richard Snow, Pat-Anthony Federico, Marshall J. Farr, and William Edward Montague. New Jersey: Lawrence Erlbaum, 1987.

Malone, Thomas Wendell. *What Makes Things Fun to Learn? A Study of Intrinsically Motivating Computer Games*. Dissertation Abstracts International. 41–05. 1980.

Mager, Robert F. (Robert Frank). *Preparing Instructional Objectives*. Kogan Page, 1991.

Mitra, Sugata, Ritu Dangwal, Shiffon Chatterjee, Swati Jha, Ravinder S. Bisht, and Preeti Kapur. 2005. "Acquisition of Computing Literacy on Shared Public Computers: Children and the 'Hole in the Wall.'" *Australasian Journal of Educational Technology*. 21, no. 3 (2005) 407–26.

Nussbaum-Beach, Sheryl, and Lani Ritter Hall. *The Connected Educator: Learning and Leading in a Digital Age*. Bloomington, IN: Solution Tree, 2012.

"PersonalLearningNetwork."https://en.wikipedia.org/wiki/Personal_learning_ network.

Richardson, Will, and Rob Mancabelli. *Personal Learning Networks: Using the Power of Connections to Transform Education*. Bloomington, IN: Solution Tree, 2011.

Schmitz, Valerie. Interview by author, Mequon, WI, October 8, 2015.

Shaull, Richard. Introduction to Pedagogy of the Oppressed, by Paulo Friere. New York: Bloomsbury, 2015.

Siemens, George. "Connectivism: A Learning Theory for the Digital Age". *International Journal of Instructional Technology and Distance Learning* (2005) http://www.itdl.org/journal/jan_05/article01.htm.

Staddon, J. E. R. *The New Behaviorism: Mind, Mechanism, and Society*. Florence, KY: Psychology, 2014.

Toffler, Alvin. *Future Shock*. New York: Bantam Books, 1996.

The Transatlantic Slave Trade Database. http://slavevoyages.org/.